401(k) Today

Another Book by
Stephen J. Butler

The Decision-Maker's Guide to 401(k) Plans

401(k) Today

Designing, Maintaining & Maximizing Your Company's Plan

Stephen J. Butler

Berrett-Koehler Publishers, Inc.
San Francisco

Berrett-Koehler Publishers, Inc.
450 Sansome Street, Suite 1200
San Francisco, CA 94111-3320
Tel: (415) 288-0260   Fax: (415) 362-2512   www.bkconnection.com

Ordering Information

Quantity sales. Special discounts are available on quantity purchases by corporations, associations, and others. For details, contact the "Special Sales Department" at the Berrett-Koehler address above.

Individual sales. Berrett-Koehler publications are available through most bookstores. They can also be ordered direct from Berrett-Koehler:
Tel: (800) 929-2929; Fax: (802) 864-7626; www.bkconnection.com

Orders for college textbook/course adoption use. Please contact Berrett-Koehler:
Tel: (800) 929-2929; Fax: (802) 864-7626.

Orders by U.S. trade bookstores and wholesalers. Please contact Publishers Group West, 1700 Fourth Street, Berkeley, CA 94710. Tel: (510) 528-1444; Fax: (510) 528-3444.

Printed in the United States of America

 Printed on acid-free and recycled paper that is composed of 50% recovered fiber, including 10% post consumer waste.

Library of Congress Cataloging-in-Publication Data
Butler, Stephen J., 1944–
    401(k) today : designing, maintaining & maximizing your company's
plan / Stephen J. Butler.
      p. cm.
    Includes bibliographical references and index.
    ISBN 1-57675-063-9 (alk. paper)
    1. 401(k) plans.   2. Pension trusts--United States.   I. Title.
HD7105.45.U6B88   1999
658.3'253--dc21   99-31554
                                                     CIP

First Edition
05 04 03 02 01 00 99   10 9 8 7 6 5 4 3 2 1

Interior Design: Gopa Design   Proofreading: Elinor Lindheimer
Editing: Marilyn Alexander   Indexing: Paula C. Durbin-Westby
Production: Linda Jupiter, Jupiter Productions

Table of Contents

Preface

I N 1995 I AUTHORED *The Decision-Maker's Guide to 401(k) Plans*, a book written to meet the needs of company owners, CFOs, human resource professionals, CPAs, and people generally charged with the decisions leading to the design and purchase of a 401(k) plan for their companies.

Since then, laws have changed and many more 401(k) plans have been started. A new book is needed to help plan sponsors improve their existing plans.

Perhaps the most important change in recent years has been the increased interest and involvement of participants in the operation of 401(k) plans. This new book is as much for plan participants as it is for plan sponsors.

The magazine *Smart Money* describes 401(k) "crusaders" who are ". . . rising up and agitating for retirement plans they can really retire on. Increasingly, across the country, participants are dictating in varying degrees how their 401(k)s will be run. Ad hoc committees are forming, and concerned employees are taking steps to influence decisions that impact their savings."[1] Margaret Mead is reported to have said, *Never doubt that a small group of thoughtful, committed citizens can change the world. Indeed, it is the only thing that ever has.*

This book is for plan participants who consider themselves to be enthusiastic, intellectually curious, and passionately committed to the opportunity of amassing real wealth, thanks to this great financial invention called the 401(k) plan. It is designed to give these centers of influence a broader understanding of 401(k)s and more clout with their plan's official decision makers.

This growing influence of plan participants puts more pressure on plan sponsors to redesign their 401(k)s to be cost effective and produce the greatest good for the greatest number of participants. This book will help plan sponsors do this.

What This Book Is About

In just four years since the first edition was published, major developments have taken place, and they can be categorized generally as follows:

1. New laws and regulations have complicated the administration of 401(k)s, but at the same time created opportunities.

2. The debate about daily versus quarterly valuation of 401(k) plan assets continues, but competitive pressures are allowing plan sponsors to negotiate lower administration costs and make daily valuation a more affordable option.

3. There is a greater public awareness of costs to 401(k) participants and plan sponsors, and there are techniques and methodologies to accurately compare costs between different 401(k) vendors.

This book discusses how 401(k) plans work and how to assess the quality of your plan and redesign it to be better. And in the process of doing this, it deals with the above three critical changes, changes with which both plan sponsors and participants must be familiar.

New 401(k) Requirements

Many new rules have been introduced in an effort to make 401(k) plans easier to administer, but exactly the reverse has happened: things are more complicated. But while there are possible new costs stemming from these changes, there are also new opportunities to deposit more money into the plans. Plans need to be redesigned to capitalize on these changes.

Part One of the book offers a basic primer on how 401(k) plans operate and how to design and administer plans based on the laws and regulations that govern them, including these new requirements, which are discussed in detail.

Plan participants, even those having a basic familiarity with 401(k) plans, will find Part One an excellent way to get a more sophisticated understanding of these plans.

For plan sponsors choosing a company's plan, the information in Part One is critical. Complicated decisions centered on plan design can have a big impact on the ease with which plans qualify for their tax-advantaged status. In many cases today, plan sponsors are left to their own devices to make these decisions, because most vendors are primarily concerned with selling their services. These vendors view the intricacies of plan design and legal compliance issues as a necessary evil, and they do not pay enough attention to them. The responsibility lies with the plan sponsor.

Daily Valuation Versus Quarterly Valuation—A New Look

The issue remains as to whether daily valuation with 800-numbers (and now Internet access) is worth what might be an extra cost. The fact is that 401(k) participants demand the service for psychological reasons. The average participant today has owned retail mutual funds in which individual service and a level of immediacy is routine. This makes it difficult for participants to understand why, in a 401(k) plan, their money may only be valued quarterly and why they have to wait several weeks after the quarter to receive their statements. Part One will discuss the advantages and disadvantages of daily and quarterly valuations.

But while daily valuation may still be more expensive, there are opportunities for plan sponsors and participants to negotiate lower administration costs through a technique called *recapture*. Part Two of the book discusses how, in effect, a 401(k) plan of any size can now be purchased *wholesale* instead of *retail*. This major change in the financial services industry is the result of extremely competitive pressures to gain a greater foothold on the lucrative 401(k) asset base. Gaining enough recapture can offset what might have been the additional costs of daily valuation.

Costs

In recent years, no subject related to 401(k) plans has received more media attention than the fees paid by plan participants and plan sponsors. There have been over 50 fee-related articles in consumer financial publications alone. Two articles by this author dealt with how vendors hide plan participant fees from plan sponsors, and how the combined costs for plan sponsors and plan participants can vary by as much as 600% from one vendor to the next.

Money magazine has estimated that the new fee awareness on the part of the American public could lead to savings of as much as $1.6 billion per year.[2] This, collectively, means trillions of extra retirement dollars in people's accounts some thirty years from now.

Part Two of this book discusses the various kinds of costs incurred by plan participants and plan sponsors. But more than that, Part Two arms participants and plan sponsors with the knowledge to compare costs and negotiate successfully with the 401(k) vendor community.

Remember, your interests may not be entirely in line with those of the financial institution operating your company's plan. So, to get the maximum benefit from your plan, it helps to understand the design decisions operating behind the scenes that can stand in the way of optimal results.

For plan participants, Part Two of this book will give the background you need to assess whether your plan is as good as possible from your perspective. With this information, you can constructively suggest to company management that they consider changes in the plan. In doing this, you would not be alone. In a growing movement across the country, there is more employee involvement in the choice of 401(k) vendors and plan provisions. In many cases, employees are forming advisory committees, or entire populations of employees are voting on the vendor selection. Informal advisory committees are forming with much the same spirit as an investment club.

For plan sponsors who are choosing vendors, investments, and design components for their company's plan, Part Two of this book will offer some valuable insight. Sorting through the marketing hype contained in the stack of three-ring binders from all the vendors is next to impossible without some organization or methodology for making an apples-to-apples comparison. Part Two contains a frank, tell-it-like-it-is story about how the industry works. It offers a simple and comprehensive technique for comparing the important differences between vendors. These tools can also be used to compute a *standard vendor cost* and then compare other vendors against it.

When the information from vendors can be accurately assessed, you can know, beyond a shadow of a doubt, that you have chosen the plan that best satisfies the combined interests of your company and its employees. By selecting the right vendor today, as your plan grows in asset size and the interests of employees become increasingly more important, you can avoid having to make a change in vendors just a few years down the road.

Testing

Another key element of 401(k) plans and one in which regulations have also changed is testing: how the 401(k) plan meets the requirements necessary for it to retain its tax-advantaged status. Part Three of the book discusses testing. It is the most complex aspect of 401(k) plans, but it may also be the most critically important. If you understand testing, not only can you avoid the tremendous cost of a plan losing its tax status, but you can design a plan that is cost effective and allows employees great flexibility in contributing money to the plan.

I have tried to make this complex subject understandable without *dumbing it down*, and I urge both plan sponsors and plan participants to read at least the first chapter in Part Three (Chapter 9), because it deals with the most basic aspect of testing. Those of you who read all of Part Three, however, will be in the best position to use testing to redesign your plan.

Finally, Part Four brings together all of the elements discussed in the book, and shows how to use them to create the ideal 401(k) plan for different kinds of organizations.

Amassing Your 401(k) Fortune

To paraphrase F. Scott Fitzgerald, *The rich are different; they have money*. Today, we can say the same about ourselves as 401(k) participants. We are different. There are over 50 million of us and we have over one trillion dollars invested in our plans. Studies indicate that we will have over five times more money at retirement than would have been the case in the absence of the 401(k) phenomenon.

Consequently, we all have an interest in information that helps us understand our plans and gauge their costs and quality. For many of us, our 401(k) plan is the most valuable asset we have. A growing percentage of us are now *401(k) millionaires*, according to *The Wall Street Journal*.[3] Substantial 401(k) account balances have changed many people's views of their work experience. There is definitely a feeling of smug satisfaction that can come from achieving financial security years before a normal retirement age.

This book gives both plan sponsors and participants the basics of 401(k) operations as well as sophisticated techniques and strategies for designing the best possible 401(k) plan. Based on my 20 years as a 401(k) plan administrator, I know that these techniques and strategies can help you become a 401(k) millionaire.

Acknowledgments

....

I WANT TO ACKNOWLEDGE my business partner, Theodore Kao, and my associates at Pension Dynamics Corporation who offer a steady stream of pension-related information that constitutes the cornerstone of this book. Ted is especially helpful with industry information, and his intuitive "ear to the ground" has helped us stay ahead of the curve as financial services trends have shifted.

Specifically, I owe a great deal to associates I have worked with for many years, including Melanie Budiman, Nicole Fornaci, Julie Sambo, Claudia Bogner, and Laura Straka. Our technical consultant, Cheryl Morgan, has made an especially valuable contribution over the years and deserves her national renown. Also, my editor, Charles Dorris, has been a major factor in helping to turn difficult subject matter into something surprisingly easy and pleasant to read.

I especially want to thank my publicist, David Graulich, for the bridges he has built to the financial press. It has been a pleasure to work together on articles that have popularized the concepts in the book. In the process, we have developed beneficial relationships with a number of key journalists for publications such as *Fortune*, *Money*, *The Wall Street Journal*, and CFO, as well as many trade and local publications. This public attention created by Mr. Graulich gave our ideas a level of exposure well beyond the circulation of the book itself.

And, finally, I want to thank my family members who have offered so much inspiration during summer vacations when the core of this book has been written. First, of course, is my wife, Fran, and my children, Elsa and Mason. Then, my parents, Elsie and William Butler, have been influential as have been my wife's parents, Fran and Mason Knox. Not to be forgotten is my sister-in-law, Marion Barthelme, a fellow writer, and Vaughan Schwarz, Ph.D., a noted psychologist. My brothers-in-law, Steve Schwarz and John Fort, have helped considerably over the years with their legal and business experience. I have a high regard and appreciation for this group's contribution to the process.

PART 1
Assessing and Redesign: Legal Considerations

WHAT THE LAW ALLOWS YOU TO DO

PART ONE OF THIS BOOK discusses the basics of the 401(k) plan that are typically dictated by tax law and pension regulations. These basics include how the plan works, how plan sponsors can contribute matching contributions to the plan, how plan participants can borrow from their plan accounts, and daily valuation of the plan's assets compared to quarterly valuation.

This material will help plan participants and plan sponsors assess and redesign their plans.

Chapter 1

Understanding How 401(k) Plans Work

THE FIRST STEP

E VERYONE INVOLVED in a 401(k) plan should be curious about how these plans work. Plan sponsors absolutely need to know. But so do plan participants. And while 401(k) plans may appear to be nothing more than a group of employees depositing money into mutual fund accounts, these plans are far more complicated. Understanding these complications defuses the frustration of employees, frustration that arises when a portion of their contributions are returned to them in some years, when they have only a limited number of investment options, and when they can't change their investment mix on any given day.

Understanding the basics of 401(k) operations also gives plan sponsors and participants the first set of building blocks that allow them to redesign the plan—to make it more cost effective and more responsive to their needs.

All basic 401(k) plans have certain characteristics:

1. Significant contributions can be made to 401(k) plans.
2. Contributions receive favorable tax treatment.
3. To qualify for their favorable tax treatment, plans must pass certain tests to assure that rank-and-file workers, as well as company owners and highly paid employees, are participating in the plan.

4. The plans are flexible and portable.
5. The plans have a relatively simple structure.
6. The plans offer professionally managed investment choices.

Significant Amounts of Money Can Be Contributed

For 1999, the maximum contribution to a 401(k) plan is 25% of a participant's annual income or $10,000, whichever is less. The dollar amount is changed periodically, based on cost-of-living adjustments.

The 25% Maximum Percentage Contribution

When I say that any one participant can contribute up to 25% of his or her annual income, this may confuse many people who have always heard that the maximum is 15%. Let me clarify this:

> For any one participant the maximum contribution is 25%, but for an entire 401(k) plan, the average percentage contribution cannot exceed 15% of the payroll for all eligible employees.

So, if in the unlikely event that all participants in a plan contributed 25%, the entire group's contribution would have to be reduced until the average for the group did not exceed 15%.

The 25% of compensation that can be contributed in behalf of a participant and the 15% of compensation that can be contributed in behalf of the entire 401(k) plan may consist of three segments:

1. The participant's contribution
2. Any employer matching contribution
3. Any employer contributions into a profit-sharing retirement plan (also called a *company discretionary contribution*)

Figure 1.1 illustrates these different segments of contributions and how the maximum percentages apply.

Two examples illustrate how this segmenting of contributions works, first, for the entire 401(k) plan and second, for one participant.

SEGMENTING 401(k) CONTRIBUTIONS

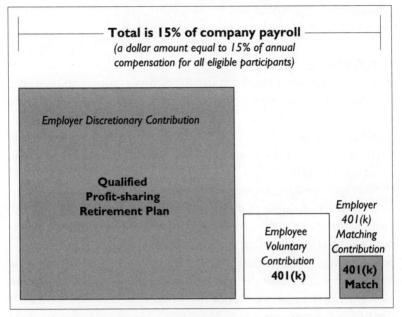

Figure 1.1

Segmenting Contributions for the Plan. To illustrate the segmenting of contributions for the entire plan, assume that contributions into the first two segments are as follows:

1. Participants make an average voluntary contribution of 6%.
2. The employer makes a matching contribution of 50 cents per $1 of the participants' average contribution; in this case that equals 3%.

With the total contributions from these two segments equaling 9%, how much can the employer contribute to the profit-sharing plan for the entire group of employees?

Because 15% of compensation is the maximum that can be contributed to all three *compartments* of the plan, the employer can contribute up to 6% (15% minus 9%) into the profit-sharing section of the plan.

Segmenting Contributions for One Participant. To illustrate the segmenting of contributions for one participant, assume that contributions into the first two segments are as follows:

1. A participant contributes 8%.
2. The employer makes a matching contribution of 50 cents per $1 of the participant's contribution; in this case that equals 4%.

Since these total 12% and the maximum contribution for a single participant is 25%, the employer could contribute up to 13% to the profit-sharing plan.

Now let's see what happens when plan and participant contributions conflict. Assume that the profit-sharing contribution for the participant above is 6%, so the total contribution for this participant is 18%. But after all of the contributions for all eligible employees is made, it's discovered that the plan's average contribution is more than 15%. Since the maximum average contribution for the plan is 15%, the plan would normally refund to the employees with the highest percentage voluntary contributions some of those contributions until an average 15% level is reached.

This sort of cutting back and fine tuning of the plan is more work for the administrator, but it offers a far better opportunity for employees than simply limiting every participant to the company's maximum 15% contribution. If that had been the case here, the participant's contribution would have been limited to 6% (instead of the 8% actually contributed), because 6% plus the 3% match plus the 6% company contribution would have totaled 15%. The participant would have missed out on additional contributions to the plan, contributions that would have produced a substantially greater 401(k) account at retirement.

The $10,000 Maximum Dollar Contribution

As mentioned earlier, for a plan participant the maximum annual contribution is 25% of annual income or $10,000. The $10,000 maximum, however, applies to the *participant's voluntary 401(k) contribution*, which is only one of the three contribution segments.

The maximum dollar amount for all three segments combined is $30,000. Many plans are now being *tweaked* as much as possible to generate contributions approaching $30,000 for owners and senior managers. We'll discuss some of these in Chapter 13.

Assessing Your Plan

The rules governing how much can be contributed are important for participants to know about, because, in many cases, they may have been told that the maximum percentage is lower than 25%. Often, for convenience purposes, the 15% maximum will be applied to individuals even when the plan as a whole is way below its average 15% maximum. This is unnecessary and penalizes many employees who would have wanted to contribute more. If you are limited to 15%, it might be wise to ask why.

Also ask:

+ Where is our plan in terms of these limits?
+ Are our plan's limits unnecessarily low to avoid extra calculations?
+ If so, what opportunity costs in future retirement benefits are we sacrificing to save a few dollars in administrative fees?
+ Is anyone connected with our plan knowledgeable about these issues or are we just buying mutual funds?

Remember, as a participant, you have a legal right to review the methods used by your company's plan governing your contributions.

Contributions to the Plan Receive Favorable Tax Treatment

Employees contribute to a 401(k) plan by voluntarily reducing their salaries and depositing money equal to the amount of the reduction into the plan. No federal or state taxes are paid on the money deposited. All investment earnings on these deposits accumulate on a tax-deferred basis.

The advantages of 401(k) plans cannot be disputed. The value of the favorable tax treatment alone is enormous. One example demonstrates this. To calculate the amount saved in the 401(k) plan, assume:

1. A participant contributes $150 per month for 20 years into a 401(k) plan.
2. The savings earn an average annual return of 8%. (This may seem high by today's standards, but during the past 60 years, the annual stock market return has averaged 10%.)
3. By the end of year 20, the savings in the plan total $88,353.

Now to calculate what a person would have saved in a regular savings plan, assume:

1. An employee saves $150 per month for 20 years.
2. The employee pays combined federal and state taxes at a rate of 34%.
3. The savings earn an annual rate of 8%.

Using after-tax dollars in a regular savings plan, the employee accumulates only $42,034. This compares to $88,353 using the 401(k) plan.

Figure 1.2 shows that these differences grow progressively larger during longer periods of time, and during a 30-year period, they become astounding. But as unbelievable as these differences seem, 401(k) plans can accomplish this feat, thanks to the magic of compound interest operating in a tax-deferred environment.

401(k) Plans Must Pass Certain Tests

In order to qualify for their favorable tax treatment of contributions and investment earnings, 401(k) plans must not discriminate against rank-and-file workers in favor of company owners, senior managers, or other highly compensated employees. If a plan does discriminate, it can be disqualified and lose its favorable tax status, as well as incur substantial penalties. To avoid disqualification, plans must pass certain discrimination tests. These tests will be covered in depth in Part Three, but let me give you some of the basics here.

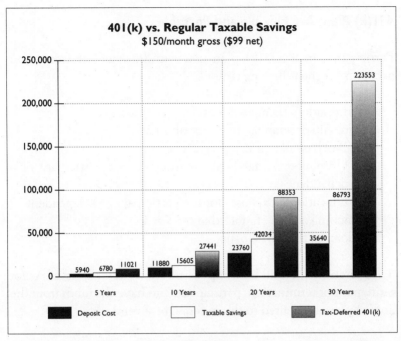

Figure 1.2

Plans start with the division of employees into two groups: those making more than $80,000 per year who are called highly compensated employees or HCEs, and those making less than $80,000 who are called non-highly compensated employees or NHCEs. The average percentage of their pay that HCEs can contribute is limited by the average percentage of pay that NHCEs contribute. In most cases, the spread between the two groups is 2%. Thus, if NHCEs contribute an average of 5% of their pay, HCEs can contribute up to an average of 7% of their pay.

In addition, if a 401(k) plan is offered, some employees can be excluded, but a certain percentage of employees must be eligible for the plan. This is verified with a *coverage* test.

Testing is a technical subject, but a critical one in designing a 401(k) plan. Those of you with a real interest in it should read Part Three now. But the intervening chapters have been written so that you don't have to tackle testing just yet.

401(k) Plans Are Flexible and Portable

Participants in a 401(k) plan can withdraw money from their accounts for the following reasons:

1. Termination of employment
2. Hardship or financial need distribution
   A. Purchase of a primary residence
   B. Unreimbursed medical expenses for the participant or a dependent
   C. Educational expenses for the participant or a dependent
3. Reaching an age of more than 59½ years
4. A loan to the participant

I'll discuss loans and hardship distributions in Chapter 2. As for retirement or termination, participants can have the funds from the 401(k) plan distributed to them in one of several ways:

1. Receive funds in a lump sum and pay regular taxes on the money.
   A If under age 59½, the participant will pay regular taxes plus federal tax penalties of 10% and (in California) state tax penalties of 2%.
   B. If over age 59½, the participant will pay regular taxes on any money taken from the plan, but no penalties.
2. Leave the funds with the former employer's 401(k) plan, if the funds total at least $5,000.
3. Roll over the funds into an IRA or into the new employer's 401(k) plan.

In options two and three, the tax obligation is further deferred, and earnings continue to build with no annual tax obligation. With the portability of 401(k) plans and the flexibility to continue deferring taxes, the participant can enjoy tax-advantaged savings for long periods of time and accumulate a large pool of capital.

401(k) Plans Have a Relatively Simple Structure

The structure of a 401(k) plan has the following building blocks:

1. A retirement plan trust
2. A plan document
3. A summary plan description for plan participants
4. The filing of an IRS form 5500 each year
5. Investment choices for the plan in keeping with U.S. Department of Labor regulation 404(c)
6. A plan sponsor

These features will be covered in great detail in later chapters, but a short description of them at this early stage may help you understand the *flesh and bones* of a 401(k) plan.

A Retirement Plan Trust Fund

This is the legal entity (much like a corporation) that houses the assets of a 401(k) plan and separates them from the money in the company that sponsors the plan. A retirement plan trust fund is controlled by trustees of the plan, who are usually the same people who own and run the company (in smaller companies anyway).

A Plan Document

This document dictates how the plan will be operated—who is eligible, matching contributions, loans, etc. The document is extremely important. An improperly signed document, for example, is a cause for plan disqualification.

A Summary Plan Description

This is the official layperson's description of the plan (as opposed to the promotional material) that, by law, must be provided to all participants. It describes, in lay terms, what the plan's general provisions are and points out that participants have the right to review all plan documents by writing to the U.S. Department of Labor in Washington, D.C.

Filing of IRS Form 5500

This is the annual report to the government that lets it keep tabs on the plan. The plan's balance sheet and income statement are reported on this form as well as the number of participants and other information regarding the plan's activity during the year. An IRS audit of the plan always centers on a review of the form 5500 for a specific year.

Investment Choices

Investment choices for the plan receive a great deal of attention, and typically conform to U.S. Department of Labor 404(c) guidelines. Generally, these investments are mutual funds, which are selected by the trustees after obtaining advice from a variety of sources.

A Plan Sponsor

The plan sponsor is the corporation or business entity that offers the plan to its employees. The plan sponsor ultimately controls all aspects and decisions of the plan not dictated by the government. The responsibilities of the plan sponsor are performed by the trustees of the plan.

Plans Offer Professionally Managed Investment Choices

Most participants wind up with better investment performance in their 401(k) plans than they would experience otherwise; there are several reasons for this.

First, the amount of money in the 401(k) plan is often substantial, enough so that the best investment advisors can be hired; advisors who are more skilled than the smaller-scale financial planners who work with individual employees.

Second, most successful business owners and senior managers, who are the trustees selecting the investments, are reasonably sophisticated. They are conscious of the fact that they are choosing investments on behalf of employees, and they have every reason to do a good job. Without a doubt, 401(k) money receives more careful consideration by decision makers than their own investments, given the *fishbowl* nature of the decision. And if these decision makers have made it this far with the company, they must have a reasonable degree of business acumen.

Third, business owners and senior managers know that a great deal is at stake: their own money is invested in the plan, and they don't want to look bad in the eyes of their employees.

The bottom line: The employee gets access to well-researched investment advice, provided with no sales commission if no-load mutual funds are the investment choices.

Summary

Both plan sponsors and plan participants must understand several basic characteristics of the 401(k) plan.

401(k) Plans Allow Substantial Contributions

- Participants can contribute the lesser of 25% of their annual compensation, or $10,000 (in 1999), which is adjusted annually based on a cost-of-living increase.

401(k) Plans Receive Favorable Tax Treatment

- Contributions to the plan reduce taxable income.
- Contributions earn income on a tax-deferred basis.
- Favorable tax treatment allows participants to accumulate savings much faster than in a regular savings account.

401(k) Plans Must Pass Certain Tests
to Receive Favorable Tax Treatment

- ◆ Plans must not discriminate against rank-and-file workers in favor of company owners and highly compensated employees. Thus, the amount that highly compensated employees can contribute as a percentage of their pay is determined by the amount contributed by non-highly compensated employees.
- ◆ Plans not passing these tests are disqualified, lose their favorable tax status, and incur substantial penalties.

401(k) Plans Are Portable

- ◆ When participants leave a company, they can
  - ◆ Be paid the account balance in a lump sum and pay taxes on the distribution.
  - ◆ Leave their 401(k) account balance with the former employer and continue to enjoy a tax-deferred treatment.
  - ◆ Roll the account balance into an IRA or the new employer's 401(k) plan and also continue to enjoy a tax-deferred treatment.

401(k) Plans Have a Legal Structure

- ◆ A *retirement trust* is established to house the plan's assets, separate from the company sponsoring the plan.
- ◆ The *plan document* specifies how the plan is to operate.
- ◆ The *plan sponsor* is the company sponsoring the plan; it is represented by a group of trustees who are usually company owners, board members, or senior managers. The plan sponsor is the plan's principal decision maker.

401(k) Plan Investments Are Professionally Selected

- ◆ The amount of money in the plan is often enough to attract the best investment advisors.
- ◆ Company owners, senior managers, and investment advisors select investments for the plan.

Chapter 2

Loans and Matching
Contributions

THE MOST UNDERRATED AND
OVERRATED ELEMENTS OF A 401(k)

CHAPTER 1 DISCUSSED the basic characteristics of a 401(k) plan.
This chapter discusses two additional aspects that companies
can elect to include:

1. The ability of participants to borrow from their accounts
2. Matching contributions offered by the company sponsoring
   the plan

Within the world of 401(k) plans, the conventional wisdom is
that plan participants should not borrow from their plans and that
matching contributions are essential for a successful plan. Unfortunately these attitudes end up being reflected in restrictive loan
policies and expensive, unwieldy matching contribution policies.

I completely disagree with these attitudes and policies. Plan
sponsors and plan participants, as they read this chapter, will be
surprised at the advantages of a liberal loan policy and how much
more important it is than matching contributions. And those of
you wanting to use matching contributions will learn how to create a simple and effective policy.

Employees Can Borrow

While the 401(k) plan ostensibly helps participants save for retirement, it also allows participants to borrow money from their accounts for goals short of retirement

The average 401(k) participant has more than 20 years before retirement. And eyes would glaze over in a room full of typical employees if only a retirement plan were discussed. Many in the workplace need to save for their children's college educations and down payments for homes. Some may need to save just to have a financial cushion, if they work in a cyclical industry. For these people, the loan provision removes a psychological impediment to depositing money into what would otherwise be strictly a retirement plan. This barrier is why relatively few people use IRAs to the maximum degree.

The loan provision works well because participants can focus on achieving a financial goal short of retirement itself. They use the plan to reach that interim goal, pay the loan back, and then go on to the next major financial accomplishment. Finally, they are ready for retirement, after having deposited into their accounts substantial sums of interest that would otherwise have been paid to banks in a series of loans. (The average $15,000 automobile purchase triggers bank interest payments of about $10,000 over the five-year life of the loan. As discussed below, employees pay interest on loans from 401(k) plans right back to themselves.)

By offering an avenue to achieve interim goals, the 401(k) plan can compete with the many consumer products and services that younger people are tempted to buy. Participants gain tremendous satisfaction from knowing that they are saving responsibly.

The Purpose of Loans

There is much confusion regarding the purposes for which loans are permitted, because many plans do not allow loans or limit the purposes for which they can be made; some plans allow loans only for down payments on primary residences.

To minimize the hassle factor of loans, these plans remove one of the greatest attributes of the 401(k) plan, especially from the perspective of younger employees. The law, however, is very clear:

> Participants can borrow from their 401(k) plans for any
> reason. Any limitations are at the discretion of the plan
> sponsor when choosing the design of the plan.

After participants first contribute to a plan, there is no waiting period before they can borrow from their accounts. But practically speaking there will not be enough money in the early months to justify a loan of any material amount. However, because 401(k) plans are portable, as discussed in Chapter 1, new employees who are not eligible to contribute would be eligible to roll an old 401(k) account balance into the new plan immediately. This allows them to continue any outstanding loans they had at their previous employment.

The Amount of Loans

Participants can borrow 50% of their account balances, up to a maximum loan of $50,000. There is no minimum loan amount.

Participants can, however, borrow more than 50% in some cases. If their account balances are under $10,000, for example, participants can borrow their entire vested account balances. But, to the extent that their loans exceed 50% of their account balances, they need to collateralize any excess amounts (amounts over 50%) with houses, cars, or savings accounts.

For example, a participant with an $8,000 account balance can borrow all $8,000, but $4,000 of the loan must be collateralized. Or, if a participant with a $10,000 account balance borrows $6,000, the first $5,000 (50% of $10,000) requires no collateral, but the remaining $1,000 of the $6,000 loan requires collateral. One thing to keep in mind: In any situation in which the loan balance is going to be more than 50% of the account balance, the maximum loan is $10,000.

At first glance, this expanded loan limit may not seem worth the effort, but it can significantly improve the overall contribution level of lower-paid employees. Here is the reason why. Many younger employees want to use the plan to save for down payments on homes. If they mistakenly thought that they could borrow only half of their account balances, they might forget the 401(k), pay their taxes, and save what was left in regular savings accounts—a much more tedious and less cost-effective way to save. Knowing that they can borrow their entire account balances prompts them to use the plan, which increases participation. And the greater the participation of rank-and-file employees, the greater the chance of the plan passing the discrimination tests mentioned in Chapter 1.

Interest Rates and Loan Terms

The interest rate on the loan is determined by the plan's trustees at the outset and must be comparable to the rate charged by a local financial institution for the same type of loan. Generally, the rate is about two percentage points higher than the prime rate.

The term of the loan can be a maximum of five years, and it must be fully amortized with payments at least quarterly. (In other words, no balloon payments at the end of five years are allowed.) There is one exception: if the loan is used to purchase the participant's primary residence, a term of up to 20 years is permitted. Early repayment on all loans is usually allowed.

How Loans Are Made

When a participant borrows from his or her 401(k) account, some of the participant's plan account assets are liquidated—the participant decides which investments to liquidate—and the proceeds loaned to the participant. The loan becomes an asset of the participant's account, in effect, another investment that the participant has chosen.

The interest paid on the loan is credited to the participant's account. The interest enjoys the same tax-deferred compounding as any other income from an investment in the plan. The interest is, however, not deductible by the participant for tax purposes.

Loan Repayment

Loans are typically repaid through an automatic deduction from the participant's salary, so that if the participant is working, the loan is automatically kept current.

If a loan goes into default while the participant is working for the company, very serious plan qualification problems result. Technically, a loan in default is an unauthorized withdrawal from the plan, so avoiding defaults is imperative. Insisting that all loans be repaid by automatic payroll deduction is the best insurance against this problem. As long as a participant is working, the loan is guaranteed to be kept current.

If the participant terminates employment, he or she can: 1) roll the loan into the new employer's 401(k) plan, 2) borrow conventionally to pay back the loan, or 3) take the unpaid loan balance as a portion of the 401(k) distribution. If the third option is chosen, it will be treated as income to the employee and will trigger a tax obligation. So repaying the 401(k) loan with options one or two is usually better. (Whereas a 401(k) account balance can be rolled into an IRA, loans cannot, so this is not an option.)

Loan Fees

The cost of setting up a loan ranges from $75 to $100, plus $50 per year to administer it, and an additional $200 set-up fee if collateral other than the participant's vested account balance is involved. The borrower should pay these fees; this creates a better barrier to the excessive use of loans than limiting loans by dollar amounts or any other means.

The Frequency of Loans

In practice, about 30% of participants borrow money from their accounts, but these loans only amount to 3–4% of total plan assets. What is the reason for this relatively infrequent use of loans? My best guess is that 401(k) money becomes sacrosanct in many participants' minds. They would rather borrow conventionally than tamper with their 401(k) money.

There is also the possible opportunity cost: if the participant borrows from an investment returning 12% annually and the participant pays only 8% on the loan, he or she misses out on a net 4% of return on the outstanding amount of the loan. On the other hand, if an employee is contributing to a 401(k) for the sole purpose of borrowing the money back relatively soon, that money will be invested in a money market fund. And the rate on the loan will exceed that earned from the money market fund. To some degree, the participant controls the opportunity cost, because he or she determines which investments to liquidate in order to generate proceeds for the loan.

A Flexible Loan Policy Versus Hardship Distributions

As was mentioned in Chapter 1, there are only two avenues for a participant who is still working to remove money from a 401(k) plan: borrowing or a hardship distribution.

Hardship Distributions. While loans can be for any reason, hardship or financial need distributions are limited to three *safe harbor* purposes:

1. Purchase of a primary residence
2. Educational expenses for the participant or a dependent
3. Unreimbursed medical expenses for the participant or a dependent

Apart from the safe harbor provisions, plan sponsors may elect to broaden their plan's definition of a hardship. In practice, approving hardship distributions beyond the safe harbor options can become a rubber stamp exercise, because the average plan sponsor does not want to stand between participants and their 401(k) money. This, however, can be risky, because if the IRS later determines that a distribution was not a hardship, it may disqualify the plan.

This difficult issue was discussed at a Western Pension Conference in San Francisco, where I sat on a panel with human resource professionals and lawyers from a collection of major Silicon Valley Fortune 4,000 companies. They were talking about how difficult it was to *play God*, as they struggled to determine what really qualified as a hardship distribution. Some of them elected to hear each participant's story and determine if it qualified for a hardship distribution. Was a new engine for the car that the participant used to get to work an acceptable hardship? I suggested that the best antidote to the hardship definition problem was to simply liberalize the loan provision.

The Cost of Hardship Distributions. Many participants hear the word *hardship* and naturally assume that there are no penalties or taxes associated with the distribution. Not so! Participants taking a hardship distribution will pay taxes at their highest marginal tax rate, because this distribution will be over and above what they already earn. For most participants, the combined federal and state income tax rate will be about 34% at the margin. Then, there will be a federal penalty of 10% and typically a state penalty of about 2%. The combined cost of a hardship distribution approaches 50% for most participants.

There is an additional cost. A participant who takes a hardship distribution must wait a year before making any further contributions to the plan. And once the money for the hardship distribution has been removed from the plan, it cannot be returned; future contributions are limited to the standard annual contribution.

Therefore, in addition to the taxes and penalties, the participant also incurs the opportunity cost of having removed money from the plan that could otherwise have been compounding on a tax-deferred basis.

Borrowing from a 401(k) plan is a less expensive way to access one's 401(k) account.

Letting the Free Market Work

A plan sponsor who fails to offer a liberal loan provision is only driving the participants into the expensive realm of the hardship distribution. And, as employees lose interest in the plan, they participate less, and the plan begins to fail the discrimination tests.

When this occurs, all too often the plan sponsor's knee-jerk reaction is to increase the matching contribution rather than to liberalize the loan provision. Increasing or adding a matching contribution might cost $10,000 to $20,000 a year. Liberalizing the loan provision might cost $150 for a plan amendment. The smart plan sponsor's rule of thumb is: Never tamper with the matching contribution until you've liberalized loans to the maximum.

The loan provision is a wonderful way to prevent the taxes and penalties incurred if money has to be withdrawn from the account to make a crucial expenditure; with the loan, the participant goes on achieving his or her savings goals.

And if participants pay the entire cost of the loan, why should anyone care whether they borrow or why they borrow? Let the free market handle the situation. What plan sponsor wants to play God, unless he or she just doesn't have enough to do.

Employers Can Offer Matching Contributions

The term *matching contribution* applies to any contribution that the employer makes that is based on a voluntary employee contribution. It can be a dollar-for-dollar match, or a match of some fraction of a dollar for each dollar of contributions.

As mentioned in the prior section, some of the most costly 401(k) design decisions center on matching contributions. Not only are the benefits of matching contributions on the plan difficult to measure accurately, but contrary to 401(k) mythology they are not needed for a successful 401(k) plan. Matching contributions may, however, improve 401(k) plan performance in some instances. To determine when to use matching contributions, you must understand the right and wrong reasons to offer matching contributions, and the right and wrong types of matching contributions to offer.

The Wrong Reasons for Offering Matching Contributions

Matching contributions are often mistakenly used as a form of incentive compensation and as an incentive to participate in the 401(k) plan.

Matching Contributions As Incentive Compensation. Under the basic philosophy of compensation, employees are paid because they work hard. They are paid a bonus when they work extra hard, when they develop additional skills and/or experience, or when a division or the entire company has a year of great performance. Ideally, these factors should be the only basis for any bonus or raise.

Companies with a 401(k) matching provision are effectively giving a bonus based solely on an employee's ability to contribute to a 401(k) plan, which may create an inequity. For example, two employees equally deserve a bonus, but only the one contributing to the 401(k) plan receives the matching contribution; the other employee, who may have just bought a house and has no discretionary income to contribute, loses out.

On one level then, a 401(k) matching contribution flies in the face of basic compensation strategy and common business sense.

Matching Contributions As an Incentive to Participate. The basic argument for a matching contribution is that it increases participation in the 401(k) plan and improves the possibility of passing the discrimination tests. However, many 401(k) plans with no matching provision pass their 401(k) discrimination tests, and the outcome of the tests appears unaffected by the matching contribution. Advertisers say that 50% *of what is spent on advertising is wasted, but you never know which 50%*. A match is a significant 401(k) cost component, and much of it probably goes to employees who would have contributed anyway.

The Wrong Type of Matching Contribution

When matching contributions are offered, they are often accompanied by a vesting schedule. Just like the vesting schedule in a traditional pension plan, vesting schedules with a matching contribution require the participant to stay with the company for some number of years before having the right to all of the matching contributions. If the participant leaves the company before becoming 100% vested, the non-vested portion is forfeited and credited toward future company matching expenses.

Vesting Schedules As a Way to Reduce the Cost of the Plan. On paper, vesting schedules should reduce the cost of the match over time. However, the company does not benefit from the non-vested forfeitures for at least a few years, until participants are actually forfeiting material amounts of money. In the meantime, the matching contribution is costing the full amount of the commitment. And, the forfeitures will never amount to much in a company with relatively low turnover among employees with one year or more of service.

Matching contributions are expensive, and vesting schedules do not reduce their cost significantly.

Vesting Schedules As a Creator of Problems. In fact, vesting schedules create problems. First, a matching provision with a vesting schedule is difficult to communicate to employees. In the middle of an otherwise great presentation to employees about saving taxes and saving money, it must be stated, *We interrupt this great program to point out that you forfeit money if you don't stay with the company for a certain length of time*.

Having to insert this element of negativity detracts from the momentum of the promotional effort. Vesting is difficult to describe in just a few short minutes. Some employees come away with the mistaken impression that if they don't stay with the company long enough, they forfeit some of their own 401(k) contributions.

In addition, vesting schedules result in the 401(k) plan having to pass an additional test as well as restricting the plan's ability to pass another test. These are explained in Chapter 10, but suffice it to say here, vesting schedules will make the plan sponsor's life more difficult.

The Right Reason for Offering Matching Contributions

If a company wants to offer a retirement benefit to only those employees who, by their voluntary 401(k) contributions, have demonstrated that saving for retirement is important to them, a matching contribution can meet this need.

All too often, companies spend money on conventional retirement plans that employees—especially younger ones—couldn't care less about. And, any money spent on compensation that employees don't recognize as being of value is just money wasted. At least a 401(k) matching contribution is guaranteed to be recognized and appreciated, because it is only received by employees contributing their own money to the plan.

A matching contribution is probably the most cost-effective form of company contribution to a qualified retirement plan. The only retirement plan more cost-effective is a 401(k) plan with no company matching contribution.

The Right Type of Matching Contribution

If a company wants to offer a matching contribution, probably the best formula involves a relatively small contribution that is capped at an annual dollar amount and is immediately 100% vested. This encourages as many employees as possible to use the 401(k) plan to some extent.

Using this formula, a company might contribute 25 cents for every dollar contributed by the participant; the matching contribution would be capped at an annual amount of $100. Thus, a participant depositing at least $400 would receive a matching contribution of $100.

This formula was used in a concert production company in which most stagehands and production employees made an average of $6 per hour; 87% of the employees eligible for the plan contributed at least $400 per year, because they couldn't stand the thought of leaving the $100 matching contribution on the table.

So, if a matching contribution is considered, it should be

1. Immediately 100% vested
2. Relatively small
3. Capped at an annual dollar amount per employee

These three rules keep the plan simple with costs under control.

Otherwise, the confusion and controversy surrounding matching contributions often creates a tragedy: the matching contribution becomes the *deal point* that stalls the momentum toward offering a 401(k) plan. If plan sponsors believe that a 401(k) plan without a match is a waste of time, they will rob themselves and their employees of tax deductions and tax-deferred compounding.

A *minimalist* approach to the matching contribution, such as the $100 example above, may generate higher contributions and a more popular plan at a very reasonable increased cost.

Plan sponsors must remember that once matching contributions are in place, they are difficult to change. Like any employee benefit, they become an entitlement in the eyes of the employees, and removal can hurt morale. A bad decision about matching contributions can cling to the plan like a barnacle, and generate an ongoing expense that dwarfs all other costs of the 401(k) plan.

Summary

Allowing participants to borrow from their 401(k) plans is one of the most important and yet most underrated factors in a successful plan. On the other hand, an employer matching contribution is one of the most expensive and overrated factors in a plan.

The Ability to Borrow Is Crucial to a 401(k) Plan's Success

* Loans can be made for any purpose.
* Loan amounts are 50% of the account balance up to a maximum loan of $50,000; however, participants can borrow 100% of the first $10,000 in their accounts.
* Loan interest rates are comparable to those of local financial institutions, and the loan term can be up to five years, and up to 20 years for the purchase of a primary residence.
* Without a liberal loan policy, participants who need to withdraw money from their accounts are forced to use hardship distributions, which carry draconian taxes and penalties.
* In practice, about 30% of participants borrow from their accounts, but the ability to borrow is a crucial element in the plan, especially for younger participants who are saving for financial goals short of retirement.

Matching Contributions Are Not Needed

* Matching contributions are costly and may not increase employee participation in the plan.
* Vesting schedules with matching contributions do not decrease the cost of the matching contributions. Further, they are difficult to explain to employees, and they can create the need for an additional test.
* If a matching contribution is offered, it should be immediately 100% vested, be relatively small, and be capped at an annual dollar amount per employee.

Chapter 3

Daily Versus Quarterly Valuation

IS DAILY VALUATION REALLY WORTH IT?

T HE GREATEST SINGLE buzzword to ever hit the pension business is *daily valuation*. Nothing else comes close, except perhaps the term *401(k)* itself.

This chapter discusses daily valuation and its advantages and disadvantages compared to quarterly valuation, which is the traditional method for valuing 401(k) plan assets.

If you are a participant in a quarterly valued plan, this chapter will explain why you have had the frustrating experience of seeing your returns differ from those that the mutual funds actually posted.

Quarterly Valuation Is the Traditional Approach

Regardless of whether 401(k) plan assets are valued quarterly or daily, the employees' contributions are deposited into the investments selected for the plan (the mutual funds, for example). The mutual fund maintains one account for money deposited by participants in a specific company's 401(k) plan.

The difference between quarterly and daily valuation occurs at the administrator level. Let's start with an example of a plan valued quarterly.

Assume that on January 1, Company ABC's 401(k) plan has a total investment of $94,000 in a mutual fund.

During the next quarter, the plan's participants add $1,000 each pay period for a total of $6,000. On March 31, the plan's cost basis in the mutual fund is $100,000.

Also during the quarter, the mutual fund's investments appreciate, and on March 31, the mutual fund's statement shows that the plan's account is valued at $102,500. The difference between the $102,500 value and the $100,000 cost basis constitutes a $2,500 gain. This gain can result not only from appreciation in the mutual fund's investments but also interest and dividends received from those investments.

During the quarter, the administrator has dealt with Company ABC's mutual fund investment as a single pool of money. Now at the end of the quarter, the administrator divides the $2,500 gain among the participants based upon their proportionate shares of the cost basis in the mutual fund. For example, assume that the account statement of Executive A shows a balance on January 1 of $9,400, 10% of the plan's $94,000 investment in that mutual fund. During the quarter, Executive A contributes a total of $600. On March 31, Executive A's cost basis is $10,000, still 10% of the total 401(k) investment of $100,000 in that mutual fund. Executive A receives 10% of the $2,500 gain and on March 31, has an account balance of $10,250.

Let's summarize what happens in a quarterly valued plan:

1. The administrator monitors only a single account for all of the plan's employees in a specific investment. So if a 401(k) plan has offered a choice of five mutual funds to its participants, the administrator monitors five pools of money—five accounts.
2. All of the money in each investment is accounted for in a pool until the end of the quarter.
3. At the end of the quarter, the plan's investments are balanced, and the gains or losses are calculated. (The balancing verifies that the deductions from each participant's pay equals the deposits into each investment, and the aggregate deductions from all participants equal the total placed in each investment.)
4. The gains or losses from each pooled investment are allocated

to individual participants' 401(k) accounts and are based on the participants' relative shares of each investment.

Each participant's share of a pooled 401(k) investment is based on his or her cost basis in the investment at the end of the quarter; this consists of the cost basis at the beginning of the quarter plus six contributions for the six pay periods during the quarter.

The simple arithmetic for this allocation could be done on a spreadsheet program, but pension software also *time weights* the gain or loss. In time weighting, a participant's share of gains and losses is based on how long his or her money was invested. For example, a participant who deposits money toward the end of the quarter does not benefit or lose from gains or losses made earlier in the quarter.

The preceding steps, then, explain how quarterly valuation of a 401(k) plan works.

Daily Valuation Is the Hot Newcomer

In a 401(k) plan that is valued daily, the employees' contributions are deposited into the investment and maintained as one account for the total plan, the same approach as used in plans that are valued quarterly. However, the administrator, instead of also maintaining a single account for all of the plan's employees until the end of the quarter, maintains an account for each participant and revalues that account daily, based on the change in the investment's value.

For example, assume that a pension administration firm has 500 clients (five hundred 401(k) plans) and 25,000 participants. These participants, in turn, have chosen a combined total of 50 different mutual funds. (Any one 401(k) plan will have offered five mutual fund selections, but because most plans offer different funds, these 500 client companies have chosen a total of 50 funds.) Every morning, the previous day's value per share of each mutual fund is entered into the employee database maintained by the administrator. Each participant's account will be revalued up or down, depending upon the daily change in price of the mutual fund. All accounts are essentially balanced every day so that the employee can be informed of his or her account balance on a daily basis. Hence the term, *daily valuation*.

To generate statements at the end of the quarter, the pension administration software sorts through all 25,000 participants and groups them based on which of the 500 clients they work for. Each company's participant statements are generated and mailed. Because all of the accounting for each participant has been done on an ongoing basis throughout the quarter, there is no additional time required for the cost basis calculation and gain or loss calculation done in a quarterly valuation—usually well after the end of the quarter.

Daily Valuation Is Popular and More Accurate

The advantages of daily valuation include:

1. Popularity with employees
2. More accurate and faster allocation of investment gains or losses

Greater Popularity With Employees

Compared to traditional quarterly valuation, daily valuation is definitely more popular with employees, for two reasons. First, it allows participants to know their account values and loan limits every day, to change their investment mixes on any day, and to call an 800 phone number the day after payday to find out if their contributions have been deposited.

Second, when an employee terminates participation in the plan, daily valuation allows a faster payout of the participant's account balance. If a participant leaves the plan in the middle of the quarter, he or she can be paid the account balance immediately because the account is balanced and has had investment gains or losses allocated to it daily. With plans valued quarterly, the payout occurs at the end of the quarter during which the participant left.

More Accurate Allocation of Gains and Losses

Daily valuation more accurately allocates gains or losses from investments. To understand this advantage, you must understand the shortcomings of quarterly valuations in this regard. Misallocations can occur in two instances: when the value of investments changes rapidly during a quarter; or when a participant withdraws a substantial amount of money from the plan (borrows or terminates participation) or changes the investment mix.

Rapid Changes in Value. As discussed earlier, in a plan that is valued quarterly, investment gains or losses are allocated on a time weighted basis (the length of time the participant's money has been invested during the quarter). However, this allocation assumes that these gains or losses occurred evenly throughout the quarter.

In fact, a mutual fund can gain or lose 10% or more in a few days. If a plan is valued quarterly, these *hiccups* in performance are not accurately reflected, and the gains or losses are misallocated.

Pension laws recognize that misallocations can happen, but the laws assume that the misallocations are a zero-sum game: any participant who loses a few cents of earnings today will get them back tomorrow when the next misallocation works in his or her favor. Daily valuation removes this characteristic of *earnings slosh* within a quarter.

Substantial Withdrawals of Money or Changes in Investment Mix. Misallocations of gains or losses can also occur when a substantial amount of a participant's investment is withdrawn or when the investment mix is changed.

For example, assume that a 401(k) plan includes an investment choice (an aggressive growth mutual fund) in which only the company president and Employee A have placed money. As of March 31, the president's account in this mutual fund is valued at $40,000 and Employee A's account at $10,000, for a total of $50,000.

In mid May, the president decides to borrow $40,000 from his 401(k) account, and his investment in this mutual fund is sold, and the proceeds used for the loan. However, since the last quarterly valuation on March 31, the mutual fund has dropped in value by 10%; the 401(k) plan's investment in it has declined from $50,000 to $45,000. The president receives $40,000 from the investment because that was the value of his investment as of the last quarterly valuation. But this withdrawal leaves only $5,000 in the account for Employee A.

If at the end of the next quarter, on June 30, there has been no further change in the share price of the mutual fund, the value of Employee A's account will be $5,000; Employee A has experienced a 50% loss (from $10,000 to $5,000) even though the investment itself lost only 10%.

This is an extreme example, and, in practice, one participant rarely controls a disproportionate share of any one investment. Also, it is not a problem in money market or guaranteed investments because these investments never decrease in value. And this phenomenon adversely affects the remaining participants in an investment only when that investment's value is falling, and, over long periods of time, stocks and bonds have increased in value; if an investment appreciates or produces earnings, the appreciation and earnings attributable to the money withdrawn remain in the plan, to be divided among the remaining participants in the investment. Finally, some quarterly plans, for an additional fee, will value their assets monthly, which lessens the misallocations.

But to some degree, this phenomenon is happening continually, as money, in any amount, is withdrawn from 401(k) plans with pooled funds and quarterly valuations. And even if there is appreciation, the participant withdrawing money is hurt by the misallocation. The misallocations caused by quarterly valuations may rarely be significant and may alternately help or hurt participants, but the problem is eliminated when daily valuation is used.

The Disadvantages of Daily Valuations Are Numerous

The disadvantages of daily valuations include:

1. Higher cost in most cases
2. Greater difficulty in solving problems
3. Investment decisions that follow the emotions and mood swings of Wall Street
4. Less emphasis on compliance and consulting

Higher Cost

For plans of any size, daily valuation is more expensive to administer than traditional quarterly valuation, because there is simply more work involved. As an extremely general rule, daily valuation, compared to quarterly valuation, increases annual costs by 1% of assets.

The Causes of the Higher Cost. Daily valuation creates the *mood of Wall Street* in what has traditionally been the quiet backwater of pension administration. A participant's call to request an investment change creates an immediate potential liability, until the money is moved by the next day. If for any reason the request slips through the cracks and the transfer does not occur, the participant may suffer a financial loss or an opportunity cost that the administrator or the plan sponsor must make up. When a major market move occurs, as in August 1998, for example, administrators offering daily valuations can be swamped with calls from participants, and the stage is set for possible errors.

There is a second cause of daily valuation's higher cost. With daily valuation, the entire client base of an administrator is adjusted every business day. Software and hardware systems are hardly trouble free. Any problem that might contaminate the system contaminates every single 401(k) plan in the administrator's database—not just the plans being worked on at that time. As a result, some administrators offering daily valuations adopt the axiom, *If anything can go wrong, it will.* They work on only one plan at a time rather than downloading daily mutual fund prices into all account files in a single operation. This limits the potential for contaminating all plans if a problem arises. However, it takes much more time.

Passing Through the Higher Costs. Most plans pass these additional costs on to employees, because the pass-through of this expense rarely surfaces as an issue. Even if it does, most employees would probably elect to pay the added expense and have daily valuation anyway, because of its popularity. The costly impact of expenses charged against earnings is rarely understood by rank-and-file employees. But this will be changing as the financial press hammers away at this particular point.

This, then, is an area in which the conscience and financial sophistication of the plan sponsor and the interested plan participant perform a valuable service in influencing and making the right decisions in behalf of employees.

More Hard-to-Solve Problems

Quarterly valuation is reasonably forgiving if mistakes have been made. The pool of money can be adjusted and corrected before employees are given statements. Thus, administrators and plan sponsors have a certain latitude. In contrast, daily valuation is very unforgiving: when it's bad, it's very bad. If a mistake is made, there is no pool of money to *massage*. The mistake has already been reflected in every participant's account. Often the mistake may be in one account but can't be found without reviewing every single account. For the administrator handling five hundred 401(k) plans and 25,000 participants, it's like having to balance 25,000 checking accounts to find a mistake in one account.

A client of mine once sent a check to the Janus fund with an account number on the check for his own internal record keeping. The number happened to have the same number of digits as the accounts used by Janus, and the check ended up in the Janus account of a doctor in Denver, Colorado. A daily valued system would have instantly misallocated this amount, making the mistake public. In a quarterly valued system, the mistake would have been quietly corrected.

Another plan sponsor made the mistake of issuing two checks for its year-end matching contribution, which doubled the contribution amount. By the time the mistake was discovered, hundreds of employees had received their shares of an extra $300,000, and the extra contributions had experienced gains or losses, depending on each participant's investment choices, including investment changes. Sorting through thousands of accounts to back out the $300,000 plus its gains and losses was an expensive accounting nightmare.

Because fixing the problem in a plan with daily valuation will be expensive, problem solving often degenerates into an exercise of assigning blame. All scheduled fees charged for plan administration assume that everything will run smoothly. If the plan sponsor does something incorrectly, the administrator is reluctant to allocate the time to correct the problem, unless paid an additional fee. A troubled daily valuation plan can be very costly to put back on its feet, and it is often the plan sponsor who gets stuck footing that bill.

Most plan sponsors are not entirely sure where the financial institution's responsibility ends and theirs begins. In reality, most service contracts leave the plan sponsor legally responsible for mistakes.

Investment Decisions That Follow Wall Street's Mood Swings

Daily valuation provides participants with greater flexibility to change investments, but moving money at any sign of bad economic news, or any bad news, can produce incorrect investment decisions and poor performance.

The average investor who tries to time the market almost always ends up worse off than if a buy-and-hold strategy had been used. The crash of October 19, 1987 is an excellent example: when investors bailed out of the equities markets during the three days when the market lost about 20%, they also lost out on the subsequent gains that brought equity accounts back to almost even by December 31.

As a general rule, the average layperson trying to time the market is usually going the wrong way when changing investment mix. And, daily valuations provide participants greater opportunity to guess wrong.

Less Emphasis on Compliance and Consulting

The different attitudes toward compliance and consulting between administrators who use quarterly and those who use daily valuations reflect a fundamental difference in their knowledge of how pension plans work and what is important.

Traditional administrators are usually trying to pass a series of exams sponsored by the American Society of Pension Actuaries. They appreciate the seriousness of compliance issues, and they have developed the ability to anticipate potential problems. Because the record keeping with quarterly valuations is easier and more forgiving than that with daily valuations, these administrators have the time and the emotional energy to think about more than just generating statements.

Administrators who offer daily valuation, by comparison, are paid to maintain daily balances, and they allocate less time and money to compliance and consulting. For example, a major mutual fund organization is often criticized for not clearly stating that the client is responsible for many compliance issues that are handled by a more traditional administrator. The transmission of payroll information to this fund organization is also less forgiving. It has an *our way or the highway* mentality, and employers who are used to a more user-friendly, hand-holding approach are usually disappointed in this aspect of these daily valuation programs.

This brings us to why many fund organizations, for example, do not prepare the annual form 5500; avoiding or farming out some portion of the administration to local firms is typical of the administrators offering daily valuation, because they need to sidestep responsibility for testing the plan and balancing the accounts. This sidestep, however, only adds to the cost.

When selecting plans that are daily or quarterly valued, understand what compliance and consulting assistance comes with it. And to state the obvious, make sure that you and your legal advisors carefully read the service agreement.

Making Daily Valuation Work in Small Companies

Traditionally, daily valuation has been cost effective only for 401(k) plans with at least 150–200 participants. Now, however, daily valuation can be cost effective in small plans, if all of the mutual funds offered to participants are on one *platform*. This means that all mutual funds must use one transfer agent or belong to one mutual fund family.

A transfer agent company does the grunt work for the mutual fund industry. Transfer agents keep track of the money and send out monthly statements. A typical transfer agent does this record keeping for as many as 100 different mutual fund families. If the funds in a 401(k) plan are all serviced by one transfer agent, then conceptually no money must be moved at the end of a day even though many participants had changed their investment mix using the 800 number or the Internet. In theory, all transactions would have netted out.

By comparison, if a daily valued plan offers funds that use many transfer agents, then a participant changing investments would have to wait three or four days while money is wired from one fund to another before it eventually clears and shows up again. If things can go wrong, they will, and a daily valuation approach that uses multiple transfer agents doesn't appear to work in practice. There are some daily valued plans that have been hopelessly out of balance and impossible to reconcile for over a year.

One caveat: Using mutual funds from the same family or that use the same transfer agent can result in more reasonable administration fees. But this may create an opportunity cost in the form of substandard performance. This will be discussed in Chapter 7.

A Hybrid Valuation Approach Can Be Cost Effective

In smaller companies, daily valuation can be offered within a quarterly valuation plan. Rather than investing in the mutual funds selected for the plan, a participant can open an individual account at a brokerage firm, make any investments he or she wishes at any time, and pay the additional cost of the bookkeeping. At the end of the quarter, information about the investment activity becomes part of the aggregate reporting for the plan.

This option must be offered to all participants. However, when told that the annual bookkeeping cost is, say, $500, most participants will remain with the mutual funds chosen for the plan.

However, a participant with a large account balance may find a $500 fee to be an acceptable cost for the additional flexibility, and possibly higher earnings, of investment options beyond those offered. This option adds not just daily valuation but a wider investment selection. Another hybrid middle ground is monthly valuation adopted by General Mills in 1999 for its 45,000 employee plan.

Summary

These days, whether daily valuation is worth the additional hard and soft dollar expense is the engine that drives the selection of vendors. In many ways, this choice may be analogous to the choice in buying an automobile: do we buy one with an automatic transmission or a stick shift? Automatics have been around for almost 50

years, but many buyers today still prefer a stick. It's more fuel efficient, and it allows the driver to push-start the car if the battery
dies. In other words, the stick shift is cheaper, and it offers a simple
solution to a car that won't start. This metaphor may explain why
traditional quarterly valued 401(k) plans will not be eclipsed by
daily valuation.

Daily valuation and quarterly valuation provide two very distinct
ways to *keep score* in a 401(k) plan.

Administrators Using Quarterly Valuation Organize Everything By Client Company

- The money in each investment is pooled in the name of the
  company's 401(k) plan.
- At the end of the quarter, contributions and gains or losses are
  allocated to the individual participants.

Administrators Using Daily Valuation Organize Everything By Individual Participant

- Contributions and gains or losses in each investment are allocated to each participant daily.
- At the end of the quarter, the accounts of the individual participants are aggregated in the name of their respective companies.

Daily Valuation Offers Popularity and Accuracy

- Employees can track their contributions and investment gains
  or losses daily, and can immediately be paid their account balances upon termination of their participation in the plan.
- Changes in investment values during the quarter are more accurately allocated.

Daily Valuation Involves More Cost and Difficulty

- Daily valuation requires more administrative work.
- Solving problems is more difficult, and the standard fees for
  daily valuation usually do not include solving problems

- Plan sponsors must deposit participant contributions more quickly.
- Administrators offering daily valuation focus on record keeping rather than on detecting and solving problems, and usually transfer the compliance and consulting tasks to the plan sponsor or to a local administrator.

Daily Valuation Can Be Cost Effective for Small Companies

- If all of a plan's mutual fund investments belong to the same fund family or use the same transfer agent, then daily valuation can be cost effective.

A Hybrid Daily/Quarterly Valuation Can Work for Small Companies

- All participants are offered a wider array of investment choices, if they pay the extra cost of record keeping.
- The relatively few participants interested in daily valuation can be serviced at a lower cost than if the entire plan were valued daily.
- A plan concerned about inequities created by quarterly valuations can consider paying for monthly valuations.

PART 2
Assessing and Redesign: Cost Considerations

THE FOCUS IS ON COST

PART TWO OF THIS BOOK is about the costs paid by both the plan sponsor and plan participants during the operation of a 401(k) plan:

Plan Participant Costs	Plan Sponsor Costs
Money management	Administration
Substandard investment performance	Plan disqualification

Part Two tells you how to analyze these costs so as to make the best decisions about which administrator and investment manager to choose and how to redesign the plan to be less costly and have a higher quality.

Chapter 4

Administration and Investment Management Tasks

WHO DOES WHAT?

M Y DOCTOR ONCE referred to the *Dermatologist Syndrome*. People with skin problems are rarely satisfied with the results they receive from the first dermatologist they see, so after a few weeks of treatment they move to a different dermatologist. The cycle continues until, about five dermatologists later, they find themselves back at their first dermatologist. By this time, the skin problem has pretty much gone away by itself.

The Dermatologist Syndrome is often seen in the 401(k) environment, where disappointed plan sponsors keep struggling to find the perfect plan. When the process is applied to 401(k) plans, however, the churning of investment managers and administrators can cost everyone—plan sponsors and participants—an unconscionable amount of money.

To help the plan sponsor and plan participant assess administrators and investment managers, this chapter discusses the tasks that they perform and the importance of these tasks. And since any problems in the performance of these tasks will likely be detected first in-house, the role and the importance of the in-house contact person will also be covered. This chapter provides a context for the discussion about costs in Chapters 5 and 6.

Administration Is the Nuts and Bolts of Operating a Plan

In selecting administrators, the plan sponsor must understand the tasks for which the administrators are being hired:

1. Complying with government regulations
2. Consulting on changes in plan design
3. Record keeping for individual participant accounts
4. Communicating investment information to participants

Complying With Government Regulations

Every aspect of 401(k) plan compliance must be handled properly. However, mistakes may happen and corrective action must be taken. Accounting mistakes, for example, are embarrassing, but they can usually be corrected relatively easily. And a mutual fund that has substandard performance can simply be replaced.

Compliance problems, however, can be a nightmare. Failing a nondiscrimination test and not correcting it in a timely manner can jeopardize the tax-qualification of the entire plan and also trigger substantial penalties payable by the company sponsoring the plan.

The IRS is auditing 401(k) plans more frequently. For most of the late 1980s, the *feeding trough* of IRS pension plan auditors was the overfunded and often abused defined-benefit pension plans enjoyed for years by doctors and dentists. Having milked that resource dry, the government began to aim its guns at 401(k) plans in 1990. The number of IRS auditors examining 401(k) plans has increased by a factor of five, and they are generally focusing on those plans with more than $1 million in assets. To date, these efforts are paying off as audits and voluntary compliance programs have generated almost $200 million in revenues. This is good business for the government.

Compliance, then, is that all-powerful *invisible shield* that needs constant administrative attention during the operation of a 401(k) plan. It's a subject that we'll discuss further in Chapter 7.

Consulting on Changes in Plan Design

After the plan is under way, continual changes in the workforce or the tax laws can require a *massaging* of some of the plan's basic components. This becomes an ongoing administrative task.

These simple design changes can be the most cost-effective way to solve, for example, a testing problem. Yet ongoing consulting is often the weak link in many plans that emphasize investment selection or generation of participant statements on time (such as daily valued plans).

In addition, many plan sponsors focus on the out-of-pocket expense to maintain their 401(k) plans; however, as the next two chapters will discuss, the biggest expense is often the opportunity cost of a plan that could accomplish much more for the same administrative fees. Some of the best money spent to administer a plan may be the few extra dollars used to review its design.

Record Keeping for Individual Participant Accounts

Record keeping links the individual participant's account to the pooled investment selections.

To repeat a little of what was said in Chapter 3, the individual contributions to 401(k) plans are pooled and allocated to the investments (the mutual funds, usually) offered by the plan and selected by the participants. The mutual fund company keeps no record of any individual participant; instead, for each 401(k) plan, there is a single investor, say, the *ABC Inc. 401(k) Retirement Trust*.

The administrator divides the pool of money in each mutual fund into individual accounts and allocates to each participant his or her share of earnings, gains, or losses. The administrator then prepares reports each quarter that summarize the activity in each participant's account.

Communicating Investment Information to Participants

Employee communication first educates the participant about the plan (how it operates, the tax savings, the loan provisions, the options upon termination of employment, and so on), and second, educates the participant about investments so that informed decisions can be made.

During the first few years of a 401(k) plan, communication should emphasize how the plan operates. Investment information should be almost incidental, because the participants' account balances are relatively small. As these balances grow, participants will need to know more about investments. For many participants, the $10,000 in their account may be far and away the most money they have ever saved. Short of winning the lottery, nothing triggers a thirst for investment knowledge more effectively than an ever-growing 401(k) account balance.

The In-House Contact Person

A Greek philosopher (Plato, I think) once said, *the smartest people in your legal system should be your policemen, because they are at the point where most justice takes place.* By analogy, many problems with 401(k) plans are first discovered and corrected in-house.

The in-house contact person is both the source for information to participants as well as the recipient of their complaints and questions. But in addition, the contact person in a quarterly valued plan will check payroll records to verify that the correct amount of money has been deducted from participants' pay, and then authorize and send the money to the specific mutual funds designated by each participant. And at the end of the year, the contact person, whether in a quarterly or daily valued plan, fills out the information form about the company ownership used in the 401(k) tests.

The contact person at the company sponsoring the plan must be detail and numbers oriented. Basically, the contact person should understand how payroll systems work, because much of the job's responsibility will involve payroll deductions and changes. It is necessary to also understand some of the basic rules of testing so that situations where testing will be a problem can be anticipated.

To educate the contact person, virtually all administrators have employee manuals that they provide at the outset of their relationship. These manuals usually offer comprehensive information about the operation of the plan. *Plan Sponsor* magazine is also a good resource, as is *The 401(k) Plan Answer Book* for those wanting more information. *Tax Facts*, *401(k) Advisor*, and *Pension Benefits* are also user-friendly resources, providing answers to common questions that arise during the operation of a 401(k) plan.[1]

The contact person must also have the right attitude. He or she must be interested in the 401(k) plan and want it to succeed. If the plan is viewed as a necessary evil at worst and a nuisance at best, the contact person will find solving problems to be unnecessarily difficult, and may indulge in finger pointing when problems arise.

These problems are not necessarily anyone's fault. Reasonable, intelligent, hard-working people can now and then miss details— details that can change the entire accounting or discrimination test results of a plan. Surveys now show that the single most aggravating problem experienced by human resource professionals centers on the ongoing demands of their 401(k) plans. With the right synergy, your plan need not be part of this statistic.

Plan sponsors must be aware of the trade-off between the quality of the in-house contact person and the administrator. Today, administration companies are under pressure to keep fees competitive and still offer flawless service. Yet, no matter how computerized an administration company may be, these plans demand people at all levels who can think and solve problems.

The least expensive administration usually means substandard service and expensive problems sooner or later. Yet inexpensive administration offers hard dollar savings. Many decision makers will choose the savings today and hope that they have reasonable luck and no future problems. When adopting this latter approach, having an experienced, intelligent in-house 401(k) contact person is imperative.

Without both good administrators and employer contact people, a 401(k) will be paddling upstream in its efforts to succeed.

Investment Management Is More Important Than Ever

There are two levels of investment management:
1. Investment advice
2. Money management

Investment advice involves selecting the mutual funds that will be offered to plan participants. (In almost all 401(k) plans, the investments selected are mutual funds because their formats accommodate the many small transactions for individual participants that are part of the normal operation of 401(k) plans.) Plan sponsors can be their own investment advisors and select mutual funds using information in publications and mutual fund rating services. Or plan sponsors can hire outside firms or individuals to help select the funds to be offered.

Money management involves the buying and selling of stocks and/or bonds, and keeping track on a minute-by-minute basis of every transaction. These functions are performed by the mutual funds selected as investment choices for the plan.

Money management and investment advice are becoming increasingly important because many plans have operated for fifteen years or longer, and participants now have substantial account balances. Participants are more concerned about investment management, and increasingly accost the CFO or human resources professional at the water cooler with questions regarding investment returns, or the lack of them.

Another reason for the increased importance of investment management has been compliance with Section 404(c) of ERISA.

These U.S. Department of Labor regulations stipulate that:

1. Participants in a 401(k) plan should be given account balance statements at least quarterly.
2. Participants should be able to choose from three investment types with different characteristics of risk and return: a guaranteed investment, a balanced fund, and a growth fund.
3. The plan committee or trustees should review the investments at least annually and measure them against standards of comparison for each investment category.
4. Each investment should have a written statement of objectives. (Virtually every mutual fund sold today has its objective expressed in the prospectus, so plans using mutual funds automatically meet this provision.)

Contrary to popular belief, Section 404(c) is not a law; it is simply a guideline. But if its provisions are met and a participant, disgruntled because of investment performance, sues the plan, the plan sponsor's liability is limited.

Lawsuits stemming from poor investment performance have been almost nonexistent where name-brand mutual funds have been offered as investments. Plans have been sued for producing extremely late participant statements or for vendor changes that led to losses or opportunity costs, because participants could not change investments within a reasonable time frame. In the future, however, as account balances increase and attorneys can take these cases on a contingency basis, the potential for lawsuits may increase.

While Section 404(c) calls for provisions that plans should offer anyway and that probably 85% of all 401(k) plans do offer, these provisions add an additional imperative beyond just common sense. They have focused more attention on investments, and plan sponsors must realize that selecting investments goes beyond their own personal interests.

Summary

If administration is a science, then investment management is an art. Administration involves accounting and legal functions. Administrators satisfy the client with speed, correct results, and a plan operation that complies with IRS demands.

By comparison, investment management involves the two-step process of first choosing a good investment advisor who will, in turn, help you decide on a selection of money managers (mutual funds) to offer as investment choices for your plan.

In some cases, the plan sponsor may act as his or her own investment advisor and choose the mutual fund offerings without any help. This is legal, but may not be wise.

In selecting outside firms and an in-house contact person, plan sponsors must understand the tasks each does and the importance of these tasks.

401(k) Plans Must Comply With Government Regulations

- Penalties for noncompliance are severe.
- IRS audits are increasingly frequent.

The 401(k) Plan Design Process Is Ongoing

- Changes in the workforce and tax laws may require changes in the design of the plan.
- Engaging a design consultant can be the most cost-effective way to solve problems.

Record Keeping Links the Participant With the Plan's Pooled Assets

- Record keeping translates the aggregate assets of the plan into individual participant accounts.
- Timely statements are vital to participant satisfaction.

Communication Educates Participants About the Plan and About Investing

- In the plan's early years, communication should educate participants about how the plan operates.
- After account balances become significant, communication should educate participants about investing.

The In-House Contact Person Is the First Line of Defense

- Most problems are detected and solved in-house.
- The in-house contact person must be able to think and solve problems.
- The in-house contact person becomes more important if a less qualified, but lower cost, administrator is selected.

Investment Management Consists of Money Management and Investment Advice

◆ The plan sponsors, using various sources of investment advice (usually investment advisors), select the mutual funds or other money managers.

◆ A money manager, usually a mutual fund, invests the plan's assets in the underlying stocks and bonds that comprise the mutual fund's assets.

Investment Management Is Now More Important Than Ever

◆ Larger account balances make participants more interested in investment results.

◆ Section 404(c), which recommends methods for handling investments, is focusing more attention on investment management.

Chapter 5

The Costs to
Plan Participants

THIS CHAPTER DISCUSSES the fees paid by plan participants, and Chapter 6 will discuss plan sponsor fees.

401(k) Plan Costs

	Plan Participant	Plan Sponsor
Hard Dollar Costs	Money management	Administration
Soft Dollar Costs	Substandard investment performance	Plan disqualification

Plan participant costs are sometimes referred to as *fees paid by the plan*. This can create the impression that they are paid by someone other than employees or the employer. In reality, any fee paid out of plan earnings or assets (and this will be explained shortly) is effectively paid by the participants.

There are two plan participant fees: money management costs and the cost of substandard performance. Before discussing each of these in detail, it may be helpful to draw a distinction between *soft dollar* and *hard dollar* costs.

Hard dollar costs are those that will actually be paid with 100% certainty each year—expenses incurred in the normal course of a 401(k) plan. They are spelled out beforehand, and they are not only predictable, but also quantifiable, sometimes negotiable, and subject to being *shopped around*. For plan participants, money management fees are a hard dollar cost.

By comparison, soft dollar costs are those that may or may not be paid, depending on what happens. For plan participants, the cost of substandard investment results is a soft cost. But if the plan experiences at least average investment results, which it should if properly designed, this cost will never be paid. The difference between hard and soft dollar costs is a subject we will return to during the next several chapters.

Money Management Costs: The Big Item

By far the largest cost of a 401(k) plan is the cost of money management, which is almost always paid for by the participants in the plan.

This money management cost is the cost of operating mutual funds or any pools of money that a 401(k) plan offers to its participants. These expenses include things such as the fee paid to the fund's investment advisor; legal and auditing fees; printing; and postage. In the heavily regulated world of mutual funds, the annual report of the fund will spell out the actual dollars spent on expenses.

These fees are deducted from the earnings of the mutual fund, thus reducing the fund's rate of return. This cost is usually referred to as the expense ratio—the expenses of the fund divided by the fund's total assets. Expense ratios will typically be about 1% per year. A portion of this cost is charged every day. If the expense ratio is 1%, then 1/365th of 1% will be charged against earnings each day.

The mutual funds offered by insurance companies have expense ratios, but insurance companies also charge what is called an *annuity wrap fee*. This is money deducted from a participant's account each year to cover the cost of administering and marketing the 401(k) plan. The typical wrap fee is 1% of assets under management, and this is in addition to the mutual fund's 1% expense ratio.

The Inside Story About Money Management Costs

Here are some facts about expense ratios and annuity wrap fees:

1. The plan sponsor cannot reimburse the plan for these charges. So once deducted from the mutual fund's earnings (and thus from the plan participant's account in the fund), the money, and what it might have earned, is gone forever.

   Reimbursement is not possible, because pension laws dictate that employer contributions to a plan must be made only as a percentage of the employee's annual salary or 401(k) contribution. To pay money into the plan as a percentage of someone's account balance could be discriminatory and favor higher-paid employees with large account balances.

2. Annuity wrap fees charged by insurance companies can sometimes be reduced through negotiation. In contrast, expense ratios cannot be lowered, because the legal prospectus of a mutual fund specifies the expenses, thereby casting it in concrete. Nothing can be changed except on a global basis in the mutual fund environment.

3. Money management costs are never offset by superior mutual fund performance. Looking ahead, it is impossible (and a violation of securities laws) to predict that superior investment results will offset greater costs. If anything, statistical probability indicates that higher expense ratios will tend to reduce returns.

4. Double-digit rates of return do not make expense ratios academic (as many vendors will claim). Table 5.1 illustrates the point.

   At higher rates of return, the accumulated assets are greater, and the 1% expense ratio produces a greater dollar cost. Higher market returns just make the opportunity cost that much greater.

   Bear in mind that this calculation illustrates the cost for just a $10,000 contribution, which represents the typical annual contribution from a company's key decision maker. A company with a $500,000 annual contribution from all of its employees combined will have costs exactly 50 times greater than those expressed in this example.

5. Table 5.1 also shows that the cost of annual expense ratios is magnified by the fact that this money could otherwise have been compounding on a tax-deferred basis over many future years. So it is a mistake to look at just one year's expense ratio comparison. To accurately assess the cost difference between two mutual funds, the difference in expense ratios must be compounded over time.

THE OPPORTUNITY COST OF 1%
$10,000 CONTRIBUTIONS OVER 24 PAY PERIODS

Percentage Annual Return	10 Years	20 Years	30 Years
10%	$171,178	$641,491	$1,925,836
9%	162,568	566,549	1,570,441
Cost of 1%	$ 8,610	$ 74,942	$ 355,395
15%	$232,057	$1,279,641	$6,008,782
14%	215,656	1,079,734	4,541,874
Cost of 1%	$ 16,401	$ 199,907	$1,466,908

SOURCE: Pension Dynamics Corporation

Table 5.1

The Hidden Costs of 401(k) Plans

Some money management fees are not disclosed. While the mutual fund industry is required to comply with federal disclosure laws that date back to the 1930s, the insurance industry enjoys laws which protect it from any federal jurisdiction. (The McCarron Fergusen Act, passed over 100 years ago, mandates that insurance companies will be regulated only by the states in which they do business.)

The net effect of this state of affairs is that insurance companies are not forced by law to disclose what they charge participants. A vice president of Great West Life was quoted in *Money* magazine as saying, "We don't specifically break out the annuity charge. All of our fees are netted against the performance of the investment."[1] More recently (July '98), John Hancock Life announced that it would divulge costs to participants, but only if directed to do so by plan sponsors.

The logo on the U.S. Department of Labor's stationery reads, "Protecting the Rights of American Workers." The agency decided in early 1998 to audit the fees to participants, both hidden and disclosed, of the insurance industry's 401(k) offerings. While the insurance industry may not be required to comply with federal securities statutes, they do need to meet certain requirements of the laws pertaining to federal pension regulations, over which the U.S. Department of Labor has jurisdiction. In other words, if you're going to sell a pension plan in this country, there are certain federal laws with which you need to come to terms.

The net effect of the audits has not been more federal legislation. Instead, the U.S. Department of Labor produced an advisory pamphlet for employee participants to alert them to the danger of high fees. This is available at the Internet web site www.dol.gov/dol/pwba.

Practically speaking, this will probably do more to reduce fees and create better opportunities for participants than any form of federal legislation. The *invisible hand* of supply and demand will operate far more effectively in an informed marketplace than any further legislation. The U.S. Department of Labor's approach was restrained, practical, and commendable. They really are here to help us.

Higher Costs From Proprietary Mutual Funds. Not to escape unscathed, the mutual fund industry may have a de facto hidden fee in the proprietary funds offered by mutual funds owned and operated by major brokerage firms. A Merrill Lynch fund or a Dean Witter fund, for example, may not have the same cultural constraints against trading securities that an independent fund family would have. Common sense would tell us that a fund whose parent organization is in the securities business may be trading more than the average fund, in an effort to generate trading commissions. The effort to save money on the spread or cost of a trade may be less intense than would be the case elsewhere. There are no studies indicating that these funds do better than the average fund, so we have to assume that they are used as *cash cows* for the brokerage firms that have created them.

For example, a 401(k) plan offered by Prudential will typically require that at least half of the mutual funds be chosen from Prudential's stable of proprietary funds. This will be true even when Prudential is paid a substantial amount in commissions and 12(b)-1 fees from outside fund families (12(b)-1 fees are marketing expenses). Why then would a brokerage firm insist on using its own proprietary funds unless it were making a substantial amount of hidden revenue over on the trading side of the equation, independent of the fund's stated operating costs?

In a *Forbes* article entitled "What's the Matter With Brokers' Funds?" the problem of poor performance was attributed to two facts: "One is that the whole psyche of a brokerage firm is built around selling, not buying. . . . Analysts at wire houses get ahead by helping underwriters, not by being skeptical. Another problem is that broker-sponsored funds tend to have steep expense ratios."[2]

The Hidden Cost From Back-End Loads. Back-end fees are incurred when money is withdrawn from a mutual fund. Many 401(k) plans are sold based on the understanding that there are no back-end loads when a participant leaves the plan, and plan sponsors thus think that there are never any such fees. Not so.

If the entire plan leaves the financial institution, the back-end load can be as high as 20%, although more often it will be between 2% and 7%. In any case, it will always be a substantial amount of money that will dwarf whatever might have been saved in administration fees by changing vendors. In all fairness, these back-end loads sometimes dissolve when plan assets reach $1 million, but many plans fall short of expectations, and assets need to be moved long before reaching that size. In other cases, they never go away.

The irony of back-end loads is that the government says they must be paid by participants rather than by the plan sponsor, unless they are excessive. As stated earlier, pension law prohibits companies from reimbursing plan participants for money management expenses. However, the government did allow a 20% back-end load to be reimbursed by one plan sponsor, and there is a fair amount of civil disobedience occurring as companies are loath to charge their participants for what turned out to be an error in judgment. This is one area where you should consider getting help from a consultant.

The Bottom Line

Paradoxically, although money management costs are the largest cost of a 401(k) plan, they are often overlooked or ignored by plan sponsors who are focused on the costs to the company. This is true even when the decision makers for the plan may have the largest account balances in the plan and may be shouldering the major portion of the expense ratio and participant cost.

While the difference between a typical 1% expense ratio and a 1.5% ratio may seem trivial, a fraction of a percent of excess costs can create a huge difference in retirement plan assets. And a retirement plan is the worst possible place to be incurring an excess cost because the extra money spent is not tax deductible (by either employer or employee). In addition, it represents missing money that could otherwise have been compounding on a tax-favored basis over many future years.

The Cost of Substandard Investments: The Sleeper

Another plan participant cost is substandard investment returns. What does this mean? The ideal 401(k) plan chooses investments from the universe of approximately 9,500 available mutual funds and winds up with five-star or A-rated funds in each investment category. (These ratings are the generally accepted indicators of quality, and they typically measure comparatively high returns with relatively low volatility.) These top-rated funds represent the standard of comparison for a 401(k) plan in a perfect world. To the extent we depart from this standard, participants begin incurring opportunity costs— the difference between their actual return and the higher return they could have achieved. How does this happen?

The Pitfalls of Packages (so-called bundled plans)

Many 401(k) plans are offered as a package with the only investments being those that the financial institutions are selling as their proprietary investments—their family of funds. Three concepts explain how this can cause substandard investment performance.

First, past history is not a guarantee of future results, but it does mean something. According to a study at the Harvard Business School, if a mutual fund outperforms its peers in a certain mutual fund category during a one-year period, it will, with a high degree of probability, continue to outperform its peers during the succeeding eight quarters. The study concluded that the top performing mutual funds consistently produced the best future performance, and the worst performing funds consistently produced the worst future performance. The study essentially proves that investment choices

derived from even the most simplistic evaluations of past performance can improve risk-adjusted returns in the future.3

Second, across a broad spectrum of different investment categories
typically included in a 401(k) package, no single investment company has the best past results in each category.

Third, the mutual funds in a bundled plan are rarely changed. The
funds are there on a global basis and are offered to all participants. To
change funds can be problematic, and new U.S. Department of Labor
rules require the vendor to notify plan sponsors 120 days before a
change in investments. This allows the plan sponsors plenty of time
to change to another vendor if they are so inclined. What 401(k)
vendor in their right mind would want to trigger this thinking?

The conclusion: Over time, if a 401(k) plan uses a single fund
family in a package, it will likely underperform a plan that selects its
mutual funds from the entire available universe.

In a more recent development, financial institutions offer at least
some funds from other mutual fund families to add a veneer of impar-
tiality to their offerings. In reality, these other funds have been chosen only partly because of superior results. A second reason, as
mentioned earlier, is that they offer generous fee-splitting opportunities for the 401(k) vendor.

The Bottom Line

Substandard investment returns are a soft cost; they can be avoided.
But in far too many cases, investments are chosen from a limited
universe of possible options that leaves us looking at only the biggest
frogs in a small pond. What we really want to have offered to us as
participants are the largest frogs from the largest possible pond.

Summary

Plan participants are responsible for two 401(k) costs: money management and substandard investment performance.

Money Management Costs Are the Big Item

- Money management costs are incurred in running the mutual funds and other investments that are available to plan participants.
- Money management is a *hard dollar cost*, a cost that is predictable and incurred in the normal operation of the 401(k) plan.
- Money management costs are usually expressed as the *expense ratio* of the mutual funds, the fund's total expenses divided by total assets. A typical expense ratio is 1%. Insurance companies express their money management cost as annuity wrap fees, which can be added to the expense ratio.
- Incurring an expense ratio greater than 1% can reduce plan assets significantly, because of the effect of compounding this amount over many years on a tax-deferred basis.

Understand the Characteristics of Expense Ratios and Wrap Fees

- They are non-reimbursable by the plan sponsor.
- Insurance companies are not legally required to disclose wrap fees.
- Wrap fees may be negotiable, but expense ratios are not.
- Above-average expenses are never offset by superior investment performance, and usually cause returns to be lower.
- Because compounding magnifies the effect of expense ratios, always evaluate them over a several-year period.
- Mutual fund investment offerings can include hidden fees in the form of proprietary mutual funds that experience higher than normal expense ratios.

Substandard Investment Performance
Is Produced By a Lack of Choice

- ◆ Substandard investment performance occurs when the mutual funds in your 401(k) perform less well than the average fund.
- ◆ Substandard investment performance is caused by financial institutions not offering a wide enough selection of investments to a 401(k) plan. This often happens in so-called bundled plans.
- ◆ Substandard investment performance is a *soft dollar cost*, because if the plan is properly designed, it should not be incurred.

Chapter 6

The Costs to
Plan Sponsors

PLAN SPONSORS HAVE two kinds of costs: administration and plan disqualification:

	Plan Participant	Plan Sponsor
Hard Dollar Costs	Money management	Administration
Soft Dollar Costs	Substandard investment performance	Plan disqualification

As was explained in the prior chapter, a *hard dollar cost* is anticipated and predictable, as administrative costs are for plan sponsors. In contrast, *soft dollar costs* may or may not have to be paid. For the plan sponsor, soft costs consist of compliance costs. These are the costs associated with a 401(k) plan being out of compliance with IRS or U.S. Department of Labor laws and regulations, and then, potentially, being disqualified. If, however, the plan stays clear of any IRS or U.S. Department of Labor problems, it should not incur these soft dollar costs.

While this chapter will be especially useful to plan sponsors, it will also give plan participants wanting to influence the design of their plan a glimpse of the plan sponsor's perspective.

Administration Cost: How Much and Who Pays?

The tasks involved in plan administration were discussed in Chapter 4, but to briefly reiterate, they involve all of the chores required to operate a 401(k) and maintain the accounting for the plan. These tasks include such things as allocating participant contributions into their investment choices, generating participant statements, conducting 401(k) discrimination testing, preparing the 5500 form or government report for the plan, and preparing paperwork for loans and distributions. In addition, plans with more than 100 employees are required to have annual CPA audits.

A typical expense for administration will include a base fee of about $1,500 for the total plan and $50 per year per employee. Other fees will include the costs for paying out distributions or loan proceeds, and, in some cases, the fee will include an annual charge of 1/10th to 5/10ths of 1% of assets.

Administration is a basic commodity across the country. As discussed in Chapter 3, the focus is different between companies that administer plans on a daily valuation basis versus a standard quarterly valued plan, but the hard dollar costs are relatively uniform, because these costs reflect the hours of work that the plan requires. For a daily valued plan, a small administration firm will usually ally itself with a major financial institution, and the costs to the plan sponsor will be about the same as using a major financial institution as the administrator.

There are no economies of scale in the administration business, because even the smaller administration firms are computerized. If anything, there may be decreasing economies of scale because larger financial institutions have to build in the costs of layers and layers of management overhead for every task performed by lower-level employees. Much of the time-consuming work of administration involves following up on details and solving the inevitable problems that arise. The seamless, electronic approach to administration has eluded (and frustrated) even the largest financial institutions in this business. Nothing involving money ever works perfectly, and there are always problems to solve.

Hard dollar costs, then, are relatively straightforward, so let's focus on soft dollar costs and how to avoid them

The Cost of Plan Disqualification

When a 401(k) plan fails any of the discrimination tests discussed in Part Three of this book, it can be subject to possible disqualification. The cost of a disqualified plan is a soft dollar cost, because if the plan is well designed, it should not be disqualified or incur any costs.

Total disqualification is rare, but there are about 125 plans disqualified across the country in a typical year. When a plan is disqualified, all taxes are due and payable as if the plan had never existed. Typically, an amount equal to half the plan's assets is payable to the government.

But, instead of this option, the government is more likely to assess penalties and sanctions, after the plan sponsor has contributed the dollar amount required to correct the plan's defect. For example, assume that a company has a plan in which non-highly compensated employees (NHCEs) contribute 5% of their income. The company, however, chose to exclude a group of workers who should have been eligible for the plan. To correct the problem, the company must contribute 5% of the excluded workers' pay (or whatever percentage the NHCEs contributed) into the plan on their behalf. And the company must do this for each year that the excluded workers should have been eligible. And if this error should be caught in an IRS audit, there would be penalties on top of this, penalties that can be massive, and that are not tax deductible.

To illustrate further, during the last few years, the IRS has collected over $130 million in penalties from over 5,700 plans. This is an average of about $24,000 per plan. And in one case the sanction was $22 million; large companies are not untouchable—the IRS views them as just a larger source of possible revenues.

How Vendors Dodge Responsibility for Compliance

Most plan sponsors are blindsided by compliance-related issues because they naturally assume that their vendor is responsible. After all that talk about fiduciary responsibility and trustee responsibility, plus *one-stop shopping* for a bulletproof 401(k) package, what company decision maker would lose sleep over possible compliance liability?

In fact, compliance problems and costs are an epidemic across the financial landscape, and the people getting stuck with the bills are plan sponsors for the most part. Why?

Service Contracts With Hold Harmless Language. Major financial institutions bury *hold harmless* language in their service agreements, thereby shifting responsibility. Here are some examples:

Fidelity Service Contract
... The Employer authorizes Fidelity to perform the non-discrimination test listed in Schedule A. All other annual Internal Revenue Code tests are the responsibility of the Employer.

Putnam Funds Self-Administration Workbook
While Putnam cannot give you legal or tax advice, our professionals have prepared these instructions and work-sheets to assist you in establishing your Putnam Retirement Plan. Please remember that these instructions and worksheets are only a general guide to help you make decisions in consultations with your legal and tax advisors.

Franklin Templeton Retainer Agreement
The Employer understands that the operation of a retirement plan is a legal undertaking, and that the plan set-up services provided by Franklin Templeton are not intended to replace legal counsel which the Employer typically seeks when considering such undertakings. Franklin Templeton recommends that the Employer consult with legal and tax counsel for advice on the plan design and specifications as well as on legal and tax issues arising during the operation of the plan.

Most plan sponsors are never presented with service contracts until the new plan is well under way, often after employee meetings have been conducted and investments are in the process of being set up. At that point, it is impractical to consider other plans, and the plan sponsors are stuck with a possible nightmare, at worst, or additional annual fees for backup professional help that they never factored in when comparing the cost of different plans.

Fortune, CFO, and *Nation's Business* have all written about this problem, and it should be common knowledge. Yet new and replacement plans are installed every day, and in all too many cases, these issues are routinely ignored. Confused plan sponsors need to appreciate that fiduciary responsibility and trustee responsibility have cost virtually nothing to date when weighed against real assessed costs of compliance responsibility.

Limiting Liability. 401(k) vendors also dodge responsibility by limiting their compliance liability to the total dollars they have collected in administrative fees during the time they have been working on the plan. This could be peanuts when compared to the cost of a disqualified plan.

Avoiding Testing Responsibility. Another more subtle technique for avoiding compliance responsibility involves testing. The administrator performs the test, but the plan sponsor supplies the information for the test—analyzing raw payroll data to determine such things as which employees are eligible for the plan, and whether an adequate number of employees are eligible. So, if the test is performed incorrectly because the data is incorrect, the administrator is off the hook.

This do-it-yourself workbook and questionnaire approach shifts one of the most critical aspects of pension administration—and the one involving the greatest financial liability—to the plan sponsor.

How Plan Sponsors Can Protect Themselves

The next time a vendor's representative drones on about fiduciary liability, just direct the conversation toward compliance and a line-by-line review of their service contract. Insist on reviewing it thoroughly before moving on to the more exciting discussion about investment choices. In some cases, this approach will end the meeting and lead to more productive use of your time.

In addition, make sure that the organization professing to administer your 401(k) plan is responsible for the following:

1. Analyzing raw payroll data
2. Identifying company ownership, including any changes from year to year, and whether any family members of owners work for the company
3. Identifying key employees of the company
4. Performing a *sweep* of information to determine if company owners have acquired other companies that would constitute a controlled group of companies, which would all be required to have the same plan
5. Preparing all statements, *all* required testing, and preparation of a signature-ready 5500 reporting form. *All tests* should be defined in the service agreement to mean all tests needed to maintain the plan's tax-qualified status, as required by the applicable agencies of the U.S. government—basically the IRS and the U.S. Department of Labor. I urge you to read Part Three of this book, with its detailed discussion about testing.

Also make sure that:

1. The service agreement guarantees that the plan will be operated in compliance with all applicable regulations.
2. There is evidence of errors and omissions insurance to make sure the guarantee is worth something.

Let me also comment on what is not protection. CPA audits are required of all plans with more than 100 employees. These audits help protect the plan sponsor from charges of malfeasance and act as a second opinion on whether the accounting for the plan has been done correctly.

CPA audits, however, are confined to accounting issues only. They are looking at the dollars in the plan and making sure that they coincide with what was contributed and what the investments returned. The CPA firm is not responsible for making sure that the plan complies with IRS pension regulations. Many plan sponsors have adopted a false sense of security as a result of this common misunderstanding.

How to Cure a Problem

While the IRS has focused its efforts on auditing pension plans in recent years by quintupling the number of agents in this assignment, the U.S. Department of Labor has also stepped up its efforts to audit plans. The combination of this audit intensity has increased the probability of mistakes being discovered. However, in practice, one of the most common situations leading to the discovery of problems is the review of a current plan by a competing vendor who has been asked to review the plan as a first step toward submitting a bid. Vendors often discover each other's mistakes and point them out to plan sponsors.

When this happens, the plan sponsor can go to the IRS and ask for the opportunity to fix the problem in return for a slap on the wrist. These voluntary compliance programs, referred to as VCR (Voluntary Compliance Resolution) and CAPS (Closing Agreements Program) amount to a vehicle for approaching the IRS and groveling on the carpet. This is a much safer approach than playing audit roulette with the plan.

With the advent of these programs, attorneys are becoming increasingly involved in 401(k) plans, because in some cases an application to the IRS through its voluntary compliance program must be submitted by an attorney.

There is an alternative to enrolling in these voluntary compliance programs. Practically speaking, there is a three-year *lookback* on plans that may have had past problems. So in some cases a business decision may be made to fix the problem by reconstructing what should have taken place and just moving on.

Don't Be Distracted By Fiduciary and Trustee Liability

Too often plan sponsors are distracted from the very real issue of compliance and plan disqualification. Mistakenly they focus instead on fiduciary and trustee liability. Fiduciary liability does sound ominous; if plan sponsors make a mistake that costs plan participants money, then they have breached their duty and must pay compensation. And plan sponsors can spend a great deal of time and money trying to mitigate or eliminate it. So, let's look at the facts.

First, there is no way for a plan sponsor to avoid fiduciary liability. Even if the administration of the plan is contracted out to a financial institution or other third party, the plan sponsor is the administrator and fiduciary in the eyes of the government.

Second, to reduce fiduciary liability somewhat, the plan sponsor can contract out a portion of the responsibility on a fee-for-service basis to a Registered Investment Advisor. But remember, you are only purchasing a co-fiduciary relationship—you are only sharing the liability, because you are responsible for selecting this advisor.

Third, in the end, the best defense against lawsuits is a well-chosen group of mutual funds (that includes a money market fund), with reasonable participant expenses, and some basic investment education for employees. Under these circumstances, lawsuits have been virtually non-existent to date.

And this is why I say, "Don't be distracted by fiduciary liability." It is technically a soft dollar cost for plan sponsors, but so far its actual cost to plan sponsors has been dwarfed by the massive cost of plan disqualification.

The Bottom Line

Compliance is a critical component in any thorough analysis of cost, but it is overlooked routinely until it is too late. It requires the same mentality as the successful purchase of life insurance. You hope your family will never need it while your kids are growing up, but responsible parents make sure that they have it.

Summary

Plan sponsors are responsible for two kinds of costs: administration and plan disqualification.

Administration Cost Is a Function of Who Does What

- ◆ Administration is a hard dollar cost (predictable and incurred in the normal course of operating the plan).
- ◆ The cost of administration is a combination of fees related to the number of participants, the administrative duties performed, and the assets being administered.
- ◆ There are no economies of scale among administrators—small firms can do it as efficiently as large ones.
- ◆ In evaluating administrators, it is imperative to not only focus on fees, but to ascertain what specific duties the administrator will perform and what duties are the responsibility of the plan sponsor.

Plan Disqualification Costs Can Be Massive

- • Disqualification means that the plan loses its tax-exempt status, because it violates any of the IRS or U.S. Department of Labor regulations affecting 401(k) plans.
- ◆ The cost of plan disqualification is a soft cost, because it can be avoided by good plan design.
- ◆ The penalty for disqualification can be immediate payment of all taxes due on plan assets, as if the plan had never existed. The more typical penalty involves substantial fees.
- ◆ Auditing of plans by the IRS and the U.S. Department of Labor is becoming increasingly intense.
- ◆ If an error is discovered in the plan prior to an audit, the plan sponsor can voluntarily go to the IRS and work with them to cure the error. Or, the plan sponsor can simply cure the problem, and move on.
- ◆ The cost of plan disqualification dwarfs that of fiduciary and trustee liability, so plan sponsors should keep their focus on compliance issues.

Chapter 7

Comparing the Costs
of Different Vendors

....

HOW TO USE THE BUTLER INDEX

D IFFERENT 401(K) PROGRAMS charge varying fees to plan sponsors and to plan participants. The challenge is to systematize
these costs as much as possible, so that valid comparisons can be
made across the spectrum of 401(k) vendors.

This chapter spells out how to use the Butler Index, which we
believe has become a standard for comparing the costs of 401(k)
packages.

What Is the Butler Index?

Table 7.1 illustrates the Butler Index, using ten vendors who are
each offering a package of investments for a 401(k) plan with
$1 million in assets and 50 employees. The Index compares the
annual costs of administration, investment management, and substandard performance.

These are actual numbers (no longer current) that show the
huge differences in costs. How this information would produce
more informed decisions about selecting vendors is easy to see.

Vendor	Employer Admin. Costs	Employee Invest. Mgt. Costs	Total	Substandard Performance Cost
A	$4,250	$2,830	$7,080	$142,289
B	4,250	5,725	9,975	173,934
C	8,089	4,740	12,829	179,145
D	4,250	8,725	12,975	127,412
E	3,750	8,125	11,875	–0–
F	4,250	9,350	13,600	134,148
G	4,850	9,515	14,345	117,911
H	4,250	11,815	16,065	235,898
I	4,250	12,265	16,515	137,120
J	10,250	9,895	20,145	145,061

Table 7.1 The Butler Index

This data in current form can be purchased, and I will discuss this later in the chapter. But you can also put it together yourself. Let me first explain this do-it-yourself approach.

An Overview of the Cost Comparison Worksheet

For each vendor in the Butler Index (each mutual fund family or package of investments), a Cost Comparison Worksheet is completed. Table 7.2. shows a Cost Comparison Worksheet for Vendor A in Table 7.1.

Name of Investment Institution: Vendor A

Name of Administration Firm (if different): Administrator A

Number of Plan Participants: 50

Plan Assets: $1,000,000

Administration Costs

Base Annual Fee	$1,500
Per Participant Fee	$ 35
Administration Asset-Based Fee	0.10%

Investment Management Costs

Money Management Fee (the expense ratio)	0.283%

	Hard Dollar Costs	
	Plan Sponsor	Plan Participant

Administration Costs

Base Annual Fee	$1,500
Per Participant Fee	1,750
Administration Asset Fee	1,000
Total Plan Sponsor Costs	$4,250

Investment Management Costs

Money Management Fee	$2,830
Total Plan Sponsor and Plan Participant Hard Costs	$7,080

	Soft Dollar Costs
Substandard Investment Cost	$142,289
Total Hard and Soft Dollar Cost	$149,369

Table 7.2 The Cost Comparison Worksheet

Table 7.2 shows the completed Cost Comparison Worksheet, so now let's discuss how we went about completing it.

Completing the Worksheet's Administration Cost Section

To assemble the administration cost data, you can contact the individual vendors, or contact your plan administrator who has access to data from several vendors. (Some additional sources of this information will be discussed later.)

As you can probably surmise from Table 7.2, generating the fees is relatively straightforward: Multiply the $35 per participant fee times the 50 participants in this plan, and multiply the 0.10% asset fee times this plan's $1 million of assets. The base annual fee is a fixed charge.

Completing the Worksheet's Investment Management Cost Section

For each of the vendors in Table 7.1, investment management costs were calculated for the same group of mutual fund types—a representative sample of investments typically offered in 401(k) plans today.

For our purposes, we chose the following eight types of mutual funds:

- ◆ One Money Market Fund
- ◆ One Bond Fund or Fixed Asset Fund like a guaranteed investment contract
- ◆ Two Total Return Funds, such as Growth and Income, Equity Income, Balanced Fund, and an Asset Allocation Fund.
- ◆ Two Growth Funds—ideally offering different investment styles.
- ◆ One Aggressive Growth or Small Company Fund
- ◆ One World or International Fund

(If your 401(k) plan uses different investment types, use those.)

For each of the vendors being analyzed, we then chose the mutual fund in each of our eight fund categories that had the best performance during the previous three years. For example, we chose the best-performing Total Return Fund from Vendors A, B, C, etc. We did the same for each of the eight types of funds. (This selection criteria is consistent with how most plan sponsors would select mutual funds.) The investment management costs from this collection of mutual fund types was compared from vendor to vendor.

Allocating Plan Assets Among These Investment Types

Step two involves allocating the assets of our 401(k) plan among these mutual funds or whatever investment types we selected. For a brand new plan that is comparing vendors, we assume that the money is equally divided among these eight different funds. For an existing plan, we use the actual percentages of the money residing in each fund category, as shown in Table 7.3.

Company Name Company ABC

Number of Plan Participants 50

Plan Assets $1,000,000

Mutual Fund Type	Percentage of Total Assets
Money Market	10
Bond	10
Total Return	15
Total Return	10
Growth	15
Growth	20
Aggressive Growth	10
World	10
	100

Table 7.3 Allocating Plan Assets Among Investments

This allocation does not have to be exact. We just want these cost comparisons to reflect what the vendors charge for the fund types most popular with a given group of employees.

Calculating a Weighted Expense Ratio

In the third step, we calculate the expense ratio for each vendor's investments in total. This requires taking the expense ratio for each mutual fund and weighting it, based on how much of the plan's assets are invested in it. We thus calculate a weighted average expense ratio.

Table 7.4 shows how a weighted average expense ratio is calculated.

	Amount Invested	Expense Ratio	Weighted Expense Ratio
Fund A	$1,000	2%	1% ($1,000/$2,000 =.5 x 2%)
Fund B	500	1%	25% ($500/$2,000 =.25 x 1%)
Fund C	500	1%	25% ($500/$2,000 =.25 x 1%)
Total	$2,000		
Total Weighted Average Cost		1.5%	

Table 7.4 Weighted Average Expense Ratio

If we had taken just the average cost of the three funds, which is 1.33% (2% + 1% + 1% = 4%, divided by three funds), we would not have accurately depicted what this 401(k) plan is paying, given the popularity of the most expensive fund, Fund A. In an extreme example, if employees had put 90% of their money into Fund A (a small company fund, let's say), the comparison of costs among vendors would be even more inaccurate without weighting.

Calculating the Investment Management Cost

Once we have calculated the weighted average expense ratio, we multiply it times the total amount of money in the plan. In this example, a plan with $1 million would be charging employees 1.5% or $15,000 in the current year. This $15,000 would be put into the Cost Comparison Worksheet and then into the Butler Index. In the example in Tables 7.1 and 7.2, the weighted expense ratio was an unusually low 0.283%, which produced an investment management cost of $2,830.

Completing the Worksheet's Substandard Performance Section

In comparing the performance of investments offered by different vendors, we look at three to five years' past performance. And using this performance data, we calculate a weighted average annual performance for each vendor's investments. To do this, we first calculate the average return for each investment, as shown in Table 7.5.

Investment A Performance

Year 1	5%
Year 2	10%
Year 3	15%

Total Return: $1 × 1.05 × 1.10 × 1.15 = $1.33 or a 33% return for three years.

Average Return: 33%/3 = 11%

Table 7.5 Average Annual Rates of Return

Next, to calculate a weighted average return for a vendor's group of funds, we weight the average return on each investment by how much is invested in each one—the same approach that we applied above to arrive at the weighted average cost. This is shown in Table 7.6.

	Annual Amount Invested	Average Return	Weighted Annual Average Return
Fund A	$1,000	11%	5.5% ($1,000/$2,000 =.5 × 11%)
Fund B	500	8%	2.0% ($500/$2,000 =.25 × 8%)
Fund C	500	14%	3.5% ($500/$2,000 =.25 × 14%)
Total	$2,000		
Annual Weighted Average Return			11%

Table 7.6 Weighted Rates of Return

We calculate this weighted average annual rate of return for each vendor. The vendor with the highest return becomes the standard. If we had invested in any other vendor's group of investments, we would have suffered substandard performance, which is a soft dollar cost. (This assumes that historical performance is a good indication of future performance, which studies show it is.)

To arrive at the actual dollar cost of substandard performance, we compute the difference between the standard return and other vendors' returns. Then this annual percentage difference is multiplied by the total dollars in the plan. Or, we can assume a hypothetical amount of, say, $1 million, as was done in Table 7.1.

In Table 7.1, Vendor E had the best past performance, and so became the standard. For this reason, Vendor E has zero cost of substandard performance. Vendor A, whose costs are featured in the Cost Comparison Worksheet in Table 7.2, had a cost for substandard performance of $142,289. The average annual performance of Vendor A was about 14.23 percentage points less than Vendor E ($1,000,000 times 14.23% equals $142,289). This may seem incredibly large, but it is a function of the tremendous run up in stock market prices in recent years and the wide range of performance among funds.

The dollar cost of substandard performance is entered into the Cost Comparison Worksheet and the Butler Index.

Tips on Using the Butler Index

The Butler Index is a great tool and to use it effectively you should understand its limitations, as well how it can be automated, and where data about vendors can be accessed.

Limitations of the Butler Index

An index of costs can not be totally accurate for the following reasons:

1. Some 401(k) programs charge back-end loads or fees if the entire plan is canceled for any reason (see Chapter 5). The Butler Index does not factor in these back-end costs, because they may never be charged if the plan keeps its assets in the mutual fund forever.

2. Some vendors reimburse participants when their account balances reach $50,000 or $100,000. Great West Life, for example, whose plans can charge total expenses of over 2% per year, currently offers to contribute $400 back into the account of a participant with over $50,000. There is no way the Index can account for this.

3. Guaranteed Investment Contracts (GICs), offered as investment choices by insurance companies, guarantee a fixed rate of return for typically three to five years. Unfortunately a plan that wants to leave this package of investments must pay a *market rate adjustment*. Since it is impossible to predict whether a plan will terminate a GIC and what the market rate adjustment will be, the Index does not measure this.

4. Fees for administration normally paid by the plan sponsor can be charged at any time as an expense of the plan—that is, plan participants pay them. Many larger plans routinely do this. Smaller companies in financial trouble can often elect to do this for a year or so.

   If a plan is passing through administration costs, it will be disclosed in the Summary Annual Report of the plan, which is provided to participants by law every year. If this fee is being charged, it should be included in the Index.

5. Instead of fees to participants that are expressed as a percentage charge, some insurance company vendors have fees *charged to earnings*, for example, the earnings of the mutual fund are reduced by the fee, and there are less earnings allocated to participants. These fees can only be calculated by reviewing the accounting of the mutual fund, and determining the cost of the investment advisory expense as a percent of the fund's total assets. Practically speaking, this can be next to impossible.

6. The Butler Index does not measure the level of service and comparative plan features—qualitative factors that vary from vendor to vendor.

Automating the Butler Index

Readers are encouraged to experiment with the spreadsheet software available on diskette with this book by sending $45 to:

> Pension Dynamics Corporation
> 985 Moraga Road, Suite 210
> Lafayette, CA 94549

We are not in the software business, so we cannot offer technical support, but the spreadsheet is in Excel, and the format is self-explanatory. The data is reasonably current, and the software allows you to enter data for other vendors not included in our current universe.

Whether you use the software or create your own Butler Index, remember that in the highly competitive world of 401(k) vendors, fees, and performance are always changing. The Butler Index reflects data at only one point in time. The data is only as current as any one vendor's most recent quote and its funds' recent performance.

Assembling Data for the Butler Index

If you are preparing your own Butler Index, you can solicit quotes from vendors or ask your plan administrator for data on vendors. A related resource is a third-party administrator (TPA). A TPA allows you to construct a plan independently from any financial institution. You can choose your investments from any of the 9,500 mutual funds available today. TPAs can also help you in compliance consulting. For the name of the TPA in your area contact:

American Society of Pension Actuaries
4350 North Fairfax Drive, Suite 820
Arlington, VA 22203–1619
Telephone: 703-516-9300
Web site: www.aspa.org

Another good source of data is HR Investment Consultants in Towson, Maryland. They publish the *401(k) Provider Directory* and other materials, which catalog fee schedules and services offered by hundreds of vendors. While magazines such as CFO periodically publish lists of providers and fees, HR Investment Consultants is by far the most comprehensive with a format that offers more information than just fee schedules. This firm can be reached at:

HR Investment Consultants
305 West Chesapeake Avenue, Suite 330
Towson, MD 21204
Telephone: 410-296-1081
Web site: www.401ksource.com

Summary

The primary objective of the Butler Index is to point out the relative differences in costs between different vendors and to illustrate how those costs can be divided between participants and plan sponsors.

The Butler Index Has Three Basic Steps

♦ Identify a group of mutual fund types (that is, Growth, Small Company, and so on) that are typical of funds offered to 401(k) plans.
♦ For each vendor that you are analyzing, identify these same types of funds, that is, Vendor A's Growth Fund and Small

Company Fund, Vendor B's Growth Fund and Small Company Fund.

◆ For each vendor's group of funds, calculate the administration cost, the average expense ratio (investment management cost), and the annual amount of substandard performance.

◆ Once this data has been assembled, you can compare different vendors by each of these costs.

The Butler Index Has Several Limitations

◆ Certain costs cannot be included in the Butler Index because they cannot be measured and because it is uncertain whether they will be incurred.

◆ The Butler Index is not intended to be the final word on what vendors are charging. It is valid for that point in time when the data is assembled. Vendor costs and performance are constantly changing.

The Butler Index Can Be Made Easy

◆ If you create your own Butler Index, you can get data by contacting vendors or your plan administrator, or use a company that consults in this area.

◆ As an alternative, you can purchase software that not only automates the process, but includes cost data on approximately 20 vendors.

Chapter 8

Recapture

....

ONE WAY OF NEGOTIATING
FOR LOWER COSTS

C HAPTERS 5 AND 6 DISCUSSED the costs charged by financial
institutions to provide administration and money management services to 401(k) plans. To some degree these costs can be
reduced through negotiation, and this chapter discusses one primary bargaining chip, called *recapture.*

In judo and other forms of Asian wrestling, the point is to use
the other person's weight and power to your advantage. When
your opponent lunges, you get underneath him and flip him on his
back. To some extent, this Karate Kid element is looming large in
the 401(k) industry in the form of recapture.

Recapture takes several forms, but basically it involves a trade-
off between administration costs and money management costs. In
a typical case, a vendor offers to administer the 401(k) plan at a
lower than normal cost, or for free. In exchange the vendor
receives the investment management contract for the assets and
charges competitive expense ratios against the plan's earnings. In
other words, a portion of the cost of administration is recaptured
by the plan, without it having to give up anything.

To appreciate this trade-off between money management costs
and administration costs, let's begin by understanding better the
costs incurred by financial institutions in providing 401(k) services. Then, we can explore the various ways that recapture works.

Managing 401(k) Assets: A License to Print Money

Mutual funds make a lot of money. As an industry, they are the world's most profitable, according to studies by Morningstar. They make a pre-tax profit of almost 30%, compared to enormously profitable companies like Microsoft that make *only* 27%.

Forbes had an interesting article asking why the U.S. Justice Department was so obsessed with breaking up Microsoft when the mutual fund industry, fragmented into over 1,000 companies, makes an even higher net profit. What do you accomplish, in other words, by breaking up a company?[1]

While it is impossible to know specifically how much mutual fund and insurance companies make on administering 401(k) plans, we can piece together some evidence that leads us to believe that it is a major factor in their amazing profitability.

For example, John Bogle (the founder of Vanguard Group) points out that a large mutual fund account with, say, $50,000 or more generates a 94% profit margin.[2] And 401(k) money is always residing in large accounts, because the actual client of the financial institution is *Company ABC 401(k) Retirement Trust.* A mutual fund company is unaware of how many participant accounts are represented by that retirement plan account. They only know that they have, say, a $1 million account on which they are earning a 94% profit. The accounts of individual participants are kept separately by the mutual fund or even a third-party administrator, and the cost of that individual accounting is paid for separately by the participants or the plan sponsor.

Figure 8.1 shows how much profit a 1% expense ratio can produce when there is a 94% profit margin. Remember, the expense ratio is the expense to the plan, not to the mutual fund.

For a different slant on the same statistic, we can consider the 401(k) plan adopted by Xerox a few years ago. Given its plan's amount of money, Xerox decided to create mutual funds in-house rather than use standard funds offered by the industry. After assessing its true cost, Xerox charged that amount to participants as the annual expense ratio: 0.03% or 3/100ths of 1% for its money management services. Imagine what the mutual funds are earning with just the usual 1% expense ratio.

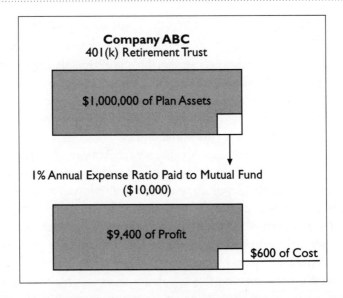

Figure 8.1 The Incredible Profitability of Mutual Funds

Why 401(k) Money Is So Profitable

Why is 401(k) money so profitable to financial institutions? There are several reasons.

First, compared to the typical 1% expense ratio paid by plan participants, the typical money management fees for traditional, large, non-401(k) pension plans have been about 0.15%. For reasons that suit the interests of the money management industry, the buyers of 401(k) plans have not been price sensitive when choosing plans. They have been more concerned with whether or not the employee educational information looks professional and whether or not participants can access account information through an 800 number, or, most recently, the Internet

Second, 401(k) money is building with new deposits every two weeks as participants contribute every pay period. Inbound money is impervious to market fluctuations. It just keeps coming like those troops in a Civil War battle. Once a financial institution has latched on to a 401(k) plan, no new advertising or marketing expenses need to be expended to generate additional contributions.

Third, 401(k) money *sticks*. While retail [non-401(k)] money is always chasing last year's best-performing mutual fund, the money in retirement plans is relatively stable. This is extremely important to money managers, because it means that they don't have to sell assets in *down* markets to redeem the shares of panicked investors. Overall, money managers will have an easier job of outperforming their competitors if they have this stable money.

Changing 401(k) investments is very cumbersome compared to a retail investor who picks up the phone and liquidates his or her account. In a 401(k) environment, all the employees must be gathered in meetings and provided with comprehensive explanations of the new plan. All of this effort and time creates a barrier to change, which suits the purposes of the incumbent financial institutions.

Finally, 401(k) assets increase exponentially in value. The fact that no taxes are paid on gains coupled with new contributions each year offers an astounding engine for increasing assets. A package sold today can reasonably be expected to double in size every three to five years. Compare this to gaining the account of someone who has retired or who has inherited some money. Those accounts are slowly liquidating themselves as opposed to increasing in value.

The 401(k) Gold Rush

This profitability fuels the frenzied efforts to sell 401(k) plans and bring that valuable money onboard. And this is reflected in how salespeople are compensated. A broker who sells a 401(k) plan receives a 1% commission on all new money coming into the mutual fund, and, from the second year on, he or she receives a yearly *trailer* fee of 0.25% of the total amount of money that has been in the account for at least one year.

If a current plan has, for example, $4 million of assets, a broker can expect to receive 1% or $40,000 for the first year *rollover* of those assets into the new plan he or she has sold. In future years, the broker will receive 0.25% or $10,000 per year on what will then be *old money*. However, presumably there is new money deposited each year estimated at, say, $500,000—which will also trigger a 1% commission or an additional $5,000.

This is why the median compensation package for someone selling these plans for a major financial institution is approximately $175,000 per year. For this, the marketing person is expected to bring in $250 million per year of new plan assets

Where does this commission money come from? In most cases, the mutual funds are effectively giving up what would have been their first year's expense ratio of about 1%. In future years, they are making enough on 401(k) annual expense ratios to pay out one quarter of this money in trailer fees.

The most important thing to remember through all of this is: Plan participants are not paying any more than what would be normal annual expense ratios. The money to pay commissions is coming from what would otherwise have been the operating revenues of the mutual fund companies. Keep this compensation formula in mind when we discuss recapture shortly.

It's easy to see why the money management industry—banks, insurance companies, and mutual funds—is so desperate to harvest 401(k) assets. And its also easy to see why the person sitting across from you in that presentable suit and sensible shoes is under a lot of pressure to sell you a plan. It's up to you to sift through the promotional hype and establish the platform of objectivity that will lead to an informed decision for yourself and your fellow employees. Millions of dollars are at stake in even the smallest of companies.

But because the investment management of 401(k) assets is so profitable, it opens the door for negotiating lower administration costs, as we shall now see.

Making Recapture Work For You

Remember, recapture is the trade-off of administration at a reduced cost, in return for investment management at a standard cost. If plan sponsors have their administration costs reduced, presumably they can afford to increase or add a matching contribution. (For participants to benefit from recapture, plan sponsors must pass along part or all of their cost savings.)

How Can This Work?

In one case, a mutual fund company offered not only free adminis-tration but up to $250,000 per year in human resource services in exchange for the privilege of taking over a major oil company's 401(k) plan.

In another situation, *heavy hitters* at some major brokerage firms who have made 401(k) plans their specialty, have been offering to pay for administration services using a portion of the substantial commissions they receive. Money that would have disappeared into the mutual fund industry has accrued to the benefit of plan sponsors and, indirectly, to participants.

In a recent California Silicon Valley situation, a company with 300 participants and $15 million of assets was shopping for a new vendor. Fidelity, Vanguard, and Schwab each offered to do the plan's annual administration at no charge. All three had comparable prod-ucts, although Vanguard's expense ratios on average were about one-third of those offered in funds from the other two vendors. Schwab was hoping that some of the participants would use its individually managed account option. So in addition to a selection of regular mutual funds chosen from Schwab's One Source universe of no-load, no-transaction-fee funds, participants would also have their own on-line brokerage account. And this would earn Schwab higher fees than the mutual fund investments chosen by participants. This case shows the trade-offs between services and costs that exist today.

Recapture Within the Mutual Fund Industry

The mutual fund industry has always been divided between so-called load and no-load funds. While all funds charge an annual expense ratio to cover their ongoing expenses, load funds also charge a com-mission payable to the brokerage community in exchange for selling their funds. No-load funds operate in an *order-taking* environment and pay no commissions to distribute their funds. They simply try to keep their expenses low and their performance above average as their primary tools for attracting new money.

Today, load funds are dropping their loads for 401(k) plans of larger sizes (typically 100-plus employees or over $1 million in assets). No-load funds, at the same time, are trying to increase their expense ratios so they can have higher margins available to pay 401(k) *packagers* like the discount brokerage firms and insurance companies.

The line is blurring between load and no-load funds when they are offered to 401(k) plans, and in both cases there are profits or marketing fees that can be applied to administration costs. In many cases, decision makers just need to know enough to ask. Subsequent negotiations can often lead to *recapture* and a more cost-effective plan.

This new trend in the industry needs to be watched carefully by plan sponsors and participants, because the interests of both can be affected dramatically and positively to the extent that they can remain ahead of the curve on these developments.

Recapture Within the Insurance Industry

With insurance company vendors, you can use a variation on recapture. Many insurance companies, such as Manufacturers Life, reduce or waive much of their fee structure for 401(k) plans beyond certain asset sizes. Also, because insurance companies are not under the strict mutual fund industry laws, they have more latitude for negotiating fees on a case-by-case basis. And since the insurance industry has been so beaten up by bad publicity in recent years about their fees, they are fighting back with competitive programs and more forthright disclosure of their costs. For these reasons, they should not be ruled out as vendors. Recapture, in this environment, is more a case of negotiating lower fees than having a vendor pay for administration or human resource services.

What to Ask For

So in negotiating with vendors and in shopping around, keep in mind the pressure points of the financial institutions, just as if you were practicing judo:

1. Salespeople may be willing to give up part of their commissions to subsidize administration costs.

2. Insurance companies have more negotiating room than mutual fund companies.

3. When a 401(k) plan has substantial assets—over $10 million— or large annual deposits—over $1 million—expect something approaching free administration in a bidding war between vendors.

4. Beyond just administration, a large plan may be able to extract even more services from a 401(k) vendor. The best service to ask for might be an airtight compliance guarantee.

The *free lunch* provided by recapture, in its various forms, is made possible by *The World's Most Profitable Industry*—mutual funds. Don't pass up a free lunch.

The Legal Underpinnings of Recapture

For a number of years, U.S. Department of Labor regulations included vague, so-called anti-kickback rules, rules that were difficult to interpret. They were clearly intended to prevent a plan sponsor from benefiting (and receiving cash) as a result of specific vendor choices for employee pension money. These regulations were an offshoot of *party-in-interest* rules that prohibit company owners or the corporation from benefiting at the expense of employees' pension accounts. The U.S. Department of Justice actually seized the assets and control of a portion of the Teamsters Union pension plan at one point because of a flood of such violations.

That was then. This is now. In the 401(k) environment, employees are given choices of investments, and they determine how their money will be invested. The opportunities for graft and corruption no longer exist. Instead, vendors or their representatives (read brokers) can offer a better deal by spending money on administration or human resource services that they would otherwise have been paid for by the plan sponsor. As long as the participants are getting a competitive deal, it boils down to how much brokers, and 401(k) vendors, want to spend or negotiate as part of their marketing effort.

The way was cleared for recapture by two U.S. Department of Labor cases. First, the Frost Bank case (Advisory Opinion 97-15A) held that Frost could offset fees it would have charged for services by whatever money it received from mutual funds included in its 401(k) package. This allowed the bank to avoid the self-dealing prohibition in ERISA Section 406(b)(1) and the anti-kickback rule in ERISA Section 406(b)(3).

In a second case involving Aetna Life Insurance Company (Advisory Opinion 97-16A), the Department of Labor also concluded that Aetna was not a fiduciary and was therefore able to collect fees from unrelated mutual funds. One key to this satisfactory outcome was the degree to which Aetna disclosed the fees it received from the funds.

Both of these cases are complex, and a close examination demands some tortured logic, but the net effect is that plan sponsors and participants can both benefit by this enlightened view of some 25-year-old laws. The days of having to worry about violating outdated anti-kickback rules appear to be over, and employers and employees can reap the benefits.

Summary

Vendors are going to elaborate lengths to gain access to 401(k) plans. There is no excuse for a plan that ignores these competitive pressures and the pricing innovations they have spawned. The invisible hand of competitive pressure is leading to better fee structures for employees as well as plan sponsors.

Recapture Is a Trade-Off

- ◆ Recapture refers to the trade-off between administration and money management costs.
- ◆ Recapture is made possible by the great profitability of the investment management industry and its highly paid salespeople.

Recapture Takes a Variety of Forms

- ◆ A vendor offers to administer a plan for a lower cost in exchange for being able to manage the plan's investments.

- ◆ A salesperson subsidizes part of the administration cost with his or her commission.
- ◆ The competition between load and no-load mutual funds can be exploited.
- ◆ The ability of insurance companies to negotiate fees and the eagerness to *get back into the game* provides competitive leverage to plan sponsors.

Recapture Is Legal

- ◆ There have been several court cases upholding the legality of recapture.

PART 3
Testing Requirements and Plan Design

....

WHERE TWO COMPLEX DISCIPLINES COME TOGETHER

PART THREE DEALS WITH the complex but critically important subject of 401(k) plan testing—those tests that must be passed in order for the plan to maintain its tax-qualified status.

This section first discusses the most basic test—the Average Deferral Percentage (ADP) Test—that all plans must pass. It next discusses several other tests that certain plans in special circumstances must pass. And finally, Part Three tells how to balance the eligibility requirements for the plan with the need to pass the tests, in order to design an optimal plan.

Chapter 9

Basic 401(k) Plan Testing

HOW TO GET A PASSING GRADE

THE AVERAGE 401(K) PARTICIPANT doesn't have a clue as to what is demanded by 401(k) testing requirements; yet, these testing requirements have been the glue that connect the interests of the company's owners with those of the employees. Why is this?

The general rationale for all pension legislation is to force or encourage company owners and top managers to offer pension plans to their employees if the owners and managers want to enjoy the benefits of these plans themselves.

To assure that lower-paid employees are not discriminated against, the 401(k) plan must pass certain discrimination tests. If the plan fails these tests, it may be disqualified, with all participants losing their tax-advantaged benefits, and the company or its owner may be assessed heavy tax penalties.

Consequently, without testing, 401(k) plans would probably have been the best-kept secret of a company's upper management, and little incentive would have existed to help employees understand the value of pre-tax dollars or a long-term investment strategy. How often, for example, did any company gather all its employees in a room to encourage them to invest in IRAs?

This chapter discusses the most basic of these discrimination tests, the Average Deferral Percentage (ADP) Test. It guarantees that the contributions of the lower-paid employees are related to those of the highly compensated employees.

The ADP Test has three steps:

1. Identify the *highly compensated employees* in the company.
2. Determine how much the *non-highly compensated employees* contributed to the plan.
3. Determine how much the highly compensated employees can contribute, using one of three formulas.

After describing how to run the test, the chapter will tell how to cure a plan that has failed, and finally, describe several refinements that can be used in running the test.

Who Are the Highly Compensated Employees?

Participants in the 401(k) plan who the IRS calls highly compensated employees or HCEs consist of two groups:

1. The owners of more than 5% of the company during either the current or the preceding year
2. Employees who earned more than $80,000 of income in the preceding year

There is an alternative way of defining an HCE, which will be discussed later in this chapter, but for the purposes of understanding the ADP Test, let's use the definitions above.

In each of these definitions, the key word is *preceding*. This generally means that it is known before the current year begins who the HCEs will be. (The exception would be an employee who becomes more than a 5% owner during the current year.)

After the HCEs have been defined, everyone else is a non-highly compensated employee or NHCE.

How Much Did Non-Highly Compensated Employees Contribute?

In running the ADP Test, first determine the percentage of compensation that non-highly compensated employees (NHCEs) contributed as a group to the 401(k) plan (for example, their average percentage).

The example in Table 9.1 illustrates how this average percentage contribution is calculated in a company with eight NHCEs.

NON-HIGHLY COMPENSATED EMPLOYEES

Participant	Salary	Dollar Contribution	Percentage Contribution
A	$10,000	$ 500	5%
B	15,000	0	0%
C	20,000	2,000	10%
D	30,000	1,500	5%
E	30,000	2,400	8%
F	40,000	800	2%
G	40,000	2,000	5%
H	45,000	2,250	5%
			Total 40%

NHCE Average Contribution 5% (40% divided by 8 employees)

Table 9.1 Calculating NHCE Percentage Contribution

After determining that the average contribution for NHCEs in this example is 5%, the next step is to determine the average contribution percentage that the HCEs will be allowed.

How Much Can Highly Compensated Employees Contribute?

There are three formulas for calculating how much highly compensated employees can contribute. The formula used in a specific case depends upon the NHCEs average percentage contribution. Was it:

1. Greater than 2% and less than 8%,
2. Less than 2%, or
3. Greater than 8%?

Greater Than 2% and Less Than 8%

If the average contribution of NHCEs is greater than 2% and less than 8% (the most common occurrence) the HCEs can contribute an average of two percentage points more than the NHCE percentage contribution.

This formula applies to the example above, because the average NHCE's contribution is 5%. The HCEs can contribute an average of two percentage points more than the NHCEs or 7% of compensation (5% plus 2%).

In the example, further assume that the company has two HCEs. Their income and contributions are shown in Table 9.2.

Participant	Salary	Dollar Contribution	Percentage Contribution
A	$ 80,000	$8,000	10%
B	120,000	4,800	4%
			Total 14%

HCE Average Contribution 7% (14% divided by 2)

Table 9.2 Calculating HCE Percentage Contributions

In this example, the test passed because the average HCE's contribution of 7% is within two percentage points of the average NHCE's contribution of 5%.

The HCEs in this example could do a little horse trading and swap percentages to some extent. If Participant A agreed to drop to an 8% contribution, then Participant B could move to 6%; their average contribution would still be 7%. All the test demands is that their average not exceed 7%.

The *plus two* formula illustrated, on the previous page, is the one most commonly used and applies when NHCEs have average contributions of between 2% and 8% of pay. The two other formulas apply when the average percentage contribution for the NHCEs is less than 2% or greater than 8%.

Less Than 2%

If the average NHCE contribution is less that 2%, the average HCE contribution is limited to double the NHCE average percentage contribution. For example, if the NHCEs contribute an average of 1.5%, the HCEs can contribute an average of not more than 3%.

More Than 8%

If the NHCE average percentage contribution is greater than 8%, the HCE average percentage contribution is limited to 1.25 times the NHCE average. So if the NHCE average contribution is 9%, the average HCE contribution can be not more than 11.25% (9% × 1.25).

Table 9.3 summarizes the relationship between the various NHCE and HCE contributions.

AVERAGE PERCENTAGE CONTRIBUTIONS

Average NHCE Contribution	Average HCE Contribution
Less than 2%	Not more than two times the NHCE contribution percentage
2% to 8%	Not more than two percentage points more than the NHCE contribution percentage
More than 8%	Not more than 1.25 times the NHCE contribution percentage

Table 9.3 Average Percentage Contributions for HCEs and NHCEs

Correcting a Failed ADP Test

If a plan fails the ADP Test, this can be corrected in one of two ways: either the amount contributed by HCEs is reduced or the amount contributed by NHCEs is increased.

First, the plan refunds HCE contributions until the plan passes. Those HCEs who have contributed the most dollars start receiving refunded contributions until the percentage for the group drops to the percentage allowed by the 2% spread (or whichever spread applies based on NHCE contribution levels). To use this option, *the money must be refunded to HCEs before the end of the year following the year in which the plan failed the test.* If the company fails to meet this deadline, it must use the second option, the QNEC.

"QNEC" (pronounced 'cue' and 'neck') stands for Qualified Non-elective Contribution. This is a contribution that the employer makes for NHCEs to increase their percentage contribution and get it in line with the HCEs' contribution percentage.

The author knows of a company with 1,500 employees that had to make an assessed QNEC cost of $400,000 after a group of HCEs had failed to receive a refund totaling $9,000 by the end of the year. QNECs are an expensive last resort. Making refunds in a timely manner is a critical plan sponsor responsibility.

Refinements to the ADP Test

In running the ADP Test, you must be aware of several refinements and recent tax law changes:

- HCEs' contributions can be increased through *negative election*.
- HCEs can be defined in an alternate way.
- All HCEs must be included in running the test.
- Either the current year's or the prior year's contributions can be used.

Increasing NHCE Contributions By Negative Election

The so-called negative election is a recently approved approach to enrolling employees in a 401(k) plan. When employees become eligible for the plan, they automatically have some percentage of salary (typically about 3%) deducted from their pay as a 401(k) deposit, unless they sign a form that prevents this from happening. In other words, the employees do not elect to join the plan, but rather, they must elect not to join the plan.

MacDonalds, for instance, has used this approach with a great deal of success. The contributions are typically deposited into a balanced fund, and employees then choose an investment mix if they want something other than a balanced mix of stocks and bonds.

For obvious psychological reasons, this approach can generate substantially higher contribution levels from some groups of employees who would otherwise struggle to determine what, if anything, they can afford to save. This approach benefits those employees as well as HCEs who can contribute more.

Refining Our Definition of Highly Compensated Employees

Tax laws passed after 1997 have presented plan sponsors with choices that they did not previously have. What they decide can have a big impact on the amount of HCE contributions that *survive* the results of testing, so it is critical for anyone concerned about their plan to think through carefully these new regulations.

Earlier in this chapter, I said that HCEs could be defined as those employees who earned more that $80,000 during the prior year. But there is an optional definition: If those employees constituted more than 20% of all employees eligible for the plan, the company can limit HCEs to 20% of all employees.

For example, if a professional firm had 100 employees eligible for the plan last year and 25 of them made more than $80,000, then the firm could define the number of HCEs as:

- ◆ All who made more than $80,000, which in this case is 25, or
- ◆ Only the top 20% of the firm's payroll, which in this case is 20.

How does a company decide which option to use? The plan sponsor runs the ADP Test twice, using each definition of HCE. Whichever definition gives the plan the best chance of passing the test is selected.

Testing is critical, and creative plan design leads to the best results. And anything short of the best results can lead to cutbacks in HCE contributions, which in turn leads to less money at retirement.

Including All HCEs

During the last year, many high income, and high contributing, employees in large firms have received surprise notices of refunds of some of their contributions. This has been caused by a change in the law that changed their status, and it probably came as a shock to those affected.

This is a classic example of why keeping up with changes in pension law is so important. In years past, the law allowed a plan to limit the number of its HCEs to 100. Now, however, there is no limit. So any employee making more than $80,000 and in the top 20% of the firm's payroll (if that optional definition is used) is an HCE.

Using the Current Year's Contributions

In running the ADP Test, you always define HCEs using their prior year's income, and determine the HCE percentage contribution by dividing their current year's contributions by their current year's income. However, to determine the NHCE percentage contribution, you can use their prior year's contribution and income or their current year's.

What are the advantages and disadvantages of using the prior or current year's numbers for NHCEs? Using the current year's numbers would certainly be more accurate—more reflective of what is actually happening. But there is a price to be paid. If we use the prior year's numbers, then on January 1 of the current year, we know for sure what the NHCEs contributed and thus what the HCEs can contribute as a percentage of their pay.

If, however, we use the current year's NHCEs contributions, we obviously won't know how much was contributed by NHCEs until the end of the year. As a result, during the year we must estimate how much NHCEs are contributing and might contribute during the rest of the year. And then probably, we must make a year-end adjustment that refunds to HCEs some of their contributions. Using the prior year's numbers offers a more predictable percentage.

Whether a plan decides to use the NHCE prior or current year's numbers must be well thought out. Beginning in 2000, whichever a plan chooses, it must live with it; no change is allowed except under restricted conditions that require five years of operation as a *current year* plan.

One last point on this. Assume that a 401(k) plan is started late this year. Next year, the plan sponsor decides to use the prior year's income and percentage contributions for NHCEs. The plan is allowed to assume that NHCEs made a *deemed 3%* contribution in the prior year, since there were no actual contributions made in the prior year. This allows HCEs to make a 5% contribution in the current year. (Since 3% is more than 2% and less than 8%, HCEs can contribute two percentage points more than NHCEs.)

However, if that new plan wants to use the current year's numbers for NHCEs, it cannot assume any contribution, but must base test results on what NHCEs actually contributed in the current year.

Summary

For the 401(k) plan to be qualified and provide tax benefits, the plan must not discriminate against lower-paid workers in favor of higher-paid workers. To enforce this rule, the government requires that the plan pass discrimination tests. Failing these tests results in the plan's disqualification, the loss of tax benefits, and possible penalties against the company sponsoring the plan.

Testing, then, is the engine that drives so many 401(k) plans. The greater the participation by rank-and-file employees, the greater the benefit to company owners and senior managers.

This need for rank-and-file participation is the rationale for allowing loans for any purpose, offering popular investment choices, promoting the plan aggressively, and allowing employees to participate after working for only a short time.

The ADP Test Is the Basic Discrimination Test

- The ADP Test assures that the contributions from highly compensated employees are based on the contributions from non-highly compensated employees.

The ADP Test Has Three Steps

- Identify who are highly compensated employees.
- Determine how much non-highly compensated employees contributed to the plan.
- Determine how much highly compensated employees can contribute. The relationships between NHCE and HCE contributions are as follows:
  - If NHCEs contribute less than 2% of pay, HCEs can contribute up to two times the NHCEs' contribution percentage.
  - If NHCEs contribute between 2% and 8% of pay, HCEs can contribute up to two percentage points more than the NHCEs' contribution percentage.
  - If NHCEs contribute more than 8% of pay, HCEs can contribute up to 1.25 times the NHCEs' contribution percentage.

If a Plan Fails, It Can Be Corrected

- To correct a failed ADP Test, a portion of the contributions are returned to the participants.

 ◆ If, however, this is not done in a timely manner, a contribution
   on behalf of all NHCEs must be made, which can be a vastly
   more expensive solution.

Several Refinements Are Allowed in Plan Design

 ◆ NHCEs can be automatically enrolled in the plan, rather than
   waiting for them to elect to join.
 ◆ HCEs can be defined in more than one way.

Chapter 10

The Specialty Testing
Required By Some Plans

I N ADDITION TO the ADP Test, described in Chapter 9, that must
be performed for all 401(k) plans, there are three other tests that
apply to some plans in special situations. The 401(m)/Multiple
Use Test and the Top-Heavy Test will be discussed in this chapter,
and the Coverage Test will be covered in Chapter 11.

The 401(m)/Multiple Use Test

In the discussion about matching contributions in Chapter 2, I
mentioned that if employees don't immediately qualify for the
entire match (if there is a vesting schedule), the plan must pass an
additional test. This is the 401(m)/Multiple Use Test.

In this test, the first step is to determine the percentage of the
matching contribution that is vested for the NHCEs. If, for example, there is a dollar-for-dollar match up to 2% of pay and a NHCE
is 50% vested, the vested matching contribution is assumed to be
1%.

Next, you determine the percentage contribution that HCEs
can make. To do this, you use one of the three formulas in Chapter 9 (see Table 9.1) that were used in the ADP Test.

But here is where it gets complicated. The HCE percentage contribution can be:

1. Double the NHCE contribution, or
2. Two percentage points more, or
3. 1.25 times more.

If you use option 3 for the 401(m)/Multiple Use Test, you can also use option 3 for the ADP Test. However, if you use options 1 or 2, you cannot use these options for the ADP Test; you must use option 3 (1.25 times) for the ADP Test.

So having a vesting schedule on the matching contribution forces the plan, in some cases, to use a less forgiving *spread* option, which costs the HCEs a significant lost opportunity to maximize their contributions.

Failing the 401(m)/Multiple Use Test can easily happen because in a typical company, HCEs are further along on the vesting schedule than the average NHCEs (where there is more turnover). Thus, plans often fail the Multiple Use Test, even if they pass the basic ADP Test. And if they fail the 401(m) Test, HCEs receive money back as taxable income.

This additional test increases administrative costs, not to mention the hassle of amended personal tax returns and the disappointment prompted by returned contributions. Moreover, the people exposed to the indignity and inconvenience of returned contributions are the last people a company wants to disappoint—its highly compensated executives.

To repeat what I said in Chapter 2, avoid matching contributions unless they are immediately 100% vested.

The Top-Heavy Test Also Limits Key Employees

In a 401(k) plan, *key* employees cannot have more than 60% of the entire assets of the plan in their accounts. If their accounts exceed 60%, the plan is *top heavy,* and if not corrected, the plan is disqualified, and participants lose all tax benefits.

Who Are Key Employees?

Key employees are not to be confused with highly compensated employees, even though the definitions are similar. Key employees consist of four groups:

+ Any officer whose annual compensation exceeds $62,500 (in 1998)
+ Each of the ten employees who own the largest percentage of the business, but excluding those who do not own more than 0.5% of the business and whose annual compensation does not exceed $30,000
+ All employees who own more than 5% of the business, regardless of annual compensation
+ All employees who own more than 1% of the business and whose annual compensation exceeds $150,000

Where Top-Heavy Problems Occur

Top-heavy problems can occur in smaller companies or in companies with many owners such as law firms. They can also occur in companies that once had traditional pension plans in which key employees built up substantial account balances. Even if the former plan was terminated four years ago and the money rolled into IRAs for the key employees, those roll-over account balances are still included in the Top-Heavy Test, thanks to a five-year *lookback* provision in the law.

Solving a Top-Heavy Problem

To solve a top-heavy problem, the company can make a top-heavy minimum contribution for all *non-key* employees of at least 3% of their annual compensation.

A second solution is to exclude the key employees from participation until their account balances become less than 60% of the entire plan's assets.

Simple math dictates the choice of solutions. If the owner(s) who would be key employees are included and are able to contribute to the plan, they will save tax dollars. How does this tax savings compare with the cost of the 3% contribution option? If the tax savings are greater than the 3% contribution, make the 3% contribution and include key employees. Otherwise, exclude them.

The Top-Heavy Test is important, but it often gets overshadowed by the basic 401(k) ADP Test. However, the top-heavy issue is becoming increasingly critical as more smaller companies offer 401(k) plans.

Safe Harbor Contributions: An Alternative to Testing

Beginning in 1999, companies can avoid testing altogether by making one of two types of company contributions into a plan:

1. A contribution to the accounts of all eligible NHCEs of 3% of their annual income, regardless of whether they are contributing to the plan
2. A two-stage matching contribution, consisting of:
   - One dollar for every dollar contributed by the NHCE up to 3% of income, plus
   - Fifty cents for every dollar contributed by the NHCE between 3% and 5% of income

The second matching option is a little complicated, so let's look at an example. Assume that an employee makes $50,000 this year and contributes 5%, $2,500. For the first 3% of the contribution ($1,500), the employee receives a dollar-for-dollar match, $1,500. For the remaining amount ($1,000), the match is fifty cents for each dollar contributed, or $500. The total matching contribution is $2,000.

Either of these company contributions must be 100% vested to qualify as the *safe harbor* provision that eliminates testing.

For most companies, this represents a significant additional expense over what they have been contributing to the plan, if anything. So it remains to be seen whether the safe harbor approach will become a trend that will reduce testing requirements across the business community.

There Are Good Reasons for Testing

Before moving into the next chapter, which completes the discussion about testing, let's consider again the rationale for a marvelous financial instrument, offering many employees one of their best opportunities to create financial security. However, to prevent disqualification of the plan and/or heavy penalties against the company sponsoring the plan, it is critical to obey the law religiously.

One look at the complex U.S. Department of Labor and IRS regulations should convince plan sponsors that the government is earnest in encouraging companies to make these plans attractive to employees. The discrimination tests required of 401(k) plans are accomplishing this purpose. They are one of the most elegant and successful attempts at social engineering ever devised by the federal government; there is now no movement to substantively change them.

Correctly performed testing is the cornerstone of a successful plan. To an extent, testing may be a nuisance and a nemesis, but plan sponsors and plan participants should appreciate that the need to pass the tests is what has made these plans so successful. Has anyone ever seen the savings plan of a company-sponsored credit union promoted as aggressively as a 401(k) plan? Surely not. It doesn't happen because it doesn't need to happen.

Summary

In addition to the ADP Test discussed in the prior chapter, a 401(k) plan may have to pass other tests if it involves a matching contribution that is not immediately 100% vested, or if the company's key employees account for more than 60% of the plan's assets. Like the ADP Test, these tests assure that lower-paid employees are not being discriminated against in favor of owners and highly paid employees.

The 401(m)/Multiple Use Test Applies to Some Plans With Matching Contributions

- ◆ If a plan includes a matching contribution that is not immediately 100% vested, this additional test is required.

◆ This test may also complicate the plan's ability to pass its ADP Test.

The Top-Heavy Test Controls Key Employees

◆ When the assets of key employees make up more than 60% of a 401(k) plan's assets, the plan is top heavy, and special limitations or regulations are triggered.
◆ A top-heavy problem can be corrected by the company contributing to the accounts of all non-key employees an amount equal to 3% of compensation.

Safe Harbor Provisions Eliminate the Need for Testing

◆ A plan can eliminate the need for testing by making one of two kinds of contributions to the plan:
  ◆ A contribution to the accounts of all eligible NHCEs of 3% of their annual income, regardless of whether they are contributing to the plan, or
  ◆ A two-stage matching contribution of one dollar for every dollar contributed up to 3% of income, plus fifty cents for every dollar contributed between 3% and 5% of income
◆ These contributions can be expensive, so plan sponsors should examine their own circumstances carefully to see if this is advantageous.

Chapter 11

Coverage Testing

DECIDING WHO
PARTICIPATES IN THE PLAN

R EMEMBER, IN RUNNING the ADP Test, all employees who are eligible for the 401(k) plan are included in the test, even those who contribute nothing. Enough of these *low contributors* can drag down the average percentage contribution for non-highly compensated employees and limit the contributions of highly compensated employees.

So if the plan is available to only employees likely to participate, it usually has a better chance of passing the ADP Test; for example, employees with several years of service are more likely to participate in a 401(k) plan than are newer employees.

The law, however, requires that a certain percentage of employees be eligible for the plan, and a Coverage Test must be passed to verify this. This chapter discusses how to balance these two objectives: passing the test and restricting eligibility to increase average contributions.

The Eligibility Period

A primary way to restrict eligibility involves the time that an employee must work before being eligible to join the plan: the eligibility period.

To participate in a 401(k) plan (to be eligible) typically requires one year of service. The employee joins the plan at the beginning of the calendar quarter following the twelfth month of service. For example, an employee who started working on August 1, 1998, would complete the twelfth month of service on July 31, 1999, and be eligible to join the plan on October 1, 1999.

If the company wants to cover only full-time employees, the twelve-month period must include at least 1,000 hours of service for the employee to qualify as full time.

When Shorter Eligibility Can Make Sense

It sometimes makes sense to choose a short eligibility period during the initial enrollment period of a brand-new 401(k) plan. During this time, everyone is talking about the plan, and there is a great deal of positive momentum. Later, as new employees become eligible one by one, that same enthusiasm is difficult to impart, and the sign-up ratios can begin to drop. When this happens, simply change to a one-year waiting period for employees hired after the initial enrollment period.

For any eligibility period shorter than one year, there is a serious complication: the 1,000 hours of service requirement can no longer be used. A plan with, for example, a 90-day eligibility period must include everyone who works even one hour per week, if they have worked 90 days.

If, for example, a company has seasonal employees who come back each year during the harvest or during the Christmas season, these employees are eligible for the plan after the first year. However, they will not be inclined to participate and will drag down the testing results. Thus, eligibility periods of less than one year can be useful, but must be used carefully.

Having championed the cause of the one-year eligibility period, I must acknowledge that some companies do just fine with shorter eligibility periods. A company that passes its ADP Test with wide margins can afford to pick whatever eligibility period it wishes. A company that is not overly concerned with the plan's administrative costs can also be more cavalier about allowing shorter-term employees to be eligible.

When Two Testing Groups at
One Company Can Be the Answer

A new wrinkle created by recent tax laws allows a company to make immediate eligibility available to all new employees. The basic 401(k) plan would be for employees with over one year of service. Then a second 401(k) plan would be for all new employees who would otherwise have been excludable until they have had a year of service. This second group is tested separately. The test will always be passed because there will never be any HCEs in this second group. Remember: To be an HCE, you have to have made more than $80,000 in the previous year. For new employees, there is no previous year. Effectively, they made zero so they will all be NHCEs no matter how much they might be paid in their first year with the company.

Depending upon when a highly compensated employee came to work, he or she could be treated as a NHCE for two full years, even if the person were making, say $10,000 per month. How? Assume a person came to work after May 1st and earned less than $80,000 the first year, and then in their second year made $120,000. The person would still be defined as a NHCE, because their earning during the first year (the prior year) was less than $80,000.

This second plan technique solves the problem that is created when you wish to offer the plan to new employees for recruiting purposes, but you do not want lower participation from this group to adversely affect the 401(k) testing.

In my experience, however, many plan problems and expenses are minimized in the long run by choosing the longest possible eligibility period. And remember, most people selling 401(k) plans have an interest in building up the number of participants. The *assumed close* in the marketing exercise is often a 90-day eligibility period. That revolving door of employees who come and go within a year may increase overall costs by as much as 20%. Look at your own company's turnover and arrive at your own estimate.

Carve-Out Techniques

In addition to the period-of-service requirement, eligibility can be restricted as to the employees covered. To exclude employees unlikely to participate, or to generally reduce the cost of the plan, companies are allowed to carve out up to 30% of their workforce. A company may want to exclude permanent part-time employees who work more than 1,000 hours per year or employees in a remote division halfway across the country. If these people are excluded, they are not considered part of the plan for testing purposes.

Understanding carve-out techniques is important, because plan sponsors are often amazed, if not blindsided, by whom they are required to include in the plan. The seasonal workers mentioned previously are one group, but even independent contractors, in some situations, can be considered part of a group controlled by the company and thus eligible for the plan.

The plan sponsor must begin to design the plan with a clear understanding of who is eligible, and then carve out groups of employees to confine the plan to those who are most likely to contribute.

The Rules of Carving Out

Section 410(b) of the Tax Code allows a retirement plan to be qualified as long as the percentage of non-highly compensated employees covered under the plan is at least 70% of the percentage of highly compensated employees covered under the plan. For example, if 100% of a company's HCEs are covered, which is typical, then 70% of the NHCEs must be covered.

Employees can be carved out as long as the plan document spells out clearly which groups of employees or which company division is being excluded. Specifically named employees cannot be carved out. Instead, for example, all clerical employees and grounds keepers can be excluded.

Carving Out Highly Compensated Employees

In most cases, a carve-out involves only non-highly compensated employees. However, Section 410(b) assumes that some employees who are carved out will be highly compensated. And, in fact, this may be in the plan's interest. For example, assume:

1. A company has ten highly compensated employees.
2. The company wants to exclude two of them because they work across the country.
3. Thus, only 80% of the company's highly compensated employees are eligible. If 80% of the highly compensated employees are eligible, the law requires that 56% (70% times 80%) of the non-highly compensated employees also be eligible.

In this example, almost half the company can be carved out, thus making it more exclusive and more likely that the plan will pass the tests. Also, the plan's administrative costs have been lowered.

In some cases, it would make economic sense to carve out a few highly compensated employees and just give them a bonus made possible by the savings generated by a more exclusive plan. Or, in some companies in which the owners are so financially well off that their 401(k) contribution is not important to them, carving them out can open the door to a more exclusive plan.

Carving Out Can Work Both Ways

In some cases, we may want to have two different plans within one company so that one part of the company can have, say, a generous matching contribution while the other portion of the same company has no match. In this case, *both* plans must pass the 410(b) Coverage Test, but this may be relatively easy.

For example in the plan above in which we had to cover at least 56% of the NHCEs in the entire company, we could have offered a second, different plan to the two executives we carved out and at least some of the 44% of the NHCEs we carved out. Since, in this second plan, we are covering 20% of the company's total HCEs (two HCEs out of ten total) we only need to cover 14% of all the company's NHCEs in this second plan (70% times 20% equals 14%).

Creative plan design uses these coverage rules liberally to accomplish customized compensation packages within a single company. It's the pension world's equivalent of laser surgery.

Carving Out Separate Lines of Business

To make the plan more exclusive, plan sponsors can use the *separate line of business* regulations. If a division or part of a company is deemed to be in a separate business from the main part of the company that is offering the 401(k) plan, the division can have its own plan or no plan at all; that is, it can be carved out.

To be deemed a separate line of business, the division to be carved out must meet the following criteria:

1. Have at least 50 employees who are eligible for the retirement plan
2. Be at least 50 miles from the main portion of the company
3. Be in a decidedly different business from that of the main part of the company

These regulations were published in final form in August 1992, but this approach to plan customization has not been used to any great extent.

Union Employees

Union employees are almost always excluded from 401(k) plans because they usually have their own union pension plans. Major league athletes, for instance, don't participate in the team's pension plan because they have their own union plans. All employees whose contracts are the product of collective bargaining fit into this category, even if they don't belong to a union.

Union employees can be included in a 401(k) plan, however, if the union itself agrees. In most cases, the union employees will not receive any matching or employer discretionary contributions. They are just allowed to make their own voluntary deposits.

Leased Employees

Employees who are leased present some of the biggest design and administrative problems in the pension world. Basically, for pension purposes, a leased employee is considered to be the same as a regular employee when the total number of leased employees represents 20% or more of your workforce. At that point, you must include the leased employees in the testing for your plan.

All too often, leased employees have not been contributing to the leasing company's plan (if it has one), and they certainly have not been part of your plan. So when they are deemed eligible for your plan, money must be deducted from their pay at the leasing company and sent to the provider of your company's plan.

Considering the administrative challenges of operating 401(k) plans without error, leased employees present a complicating factor that most plan sponsors would do well to avoid. Meanwhile, do not let anyone tell you that leased employees will not be part of your 401(k) and its testing. That is only true up to a point, and the question becomes that of who will monitor the 20% point at which the plan is subject to disqualification. In my experience, very few plan sponsors are cognizant of the potential risks to their plan from leased employees.

Being Restrictive While Accommodating New Employees

In dealing with the issue of eligibility, the thinking of plan sponsors is clouded because they want their plans to accommodate newly recruited employees. They want to say that the 401(k) plan is available, especially to new key management people.

Earlier, I suggested that a second 401(k) plan could be created for new employees. Here are some other practical and indirect ways to solve this problem and also maintain the one-year eligibility period.

First, maintain the one-year eligibility period for contributions, but allow new employees to roll over previous 401(k) account balances into your plan immediately. This allows them to use the borrowing feature of the 401(k) plan without interfering with the testing requirements.

Second, remind new employees that they have the legal right to leave their money in their prior employer's 401(k) account if they have more than $5,000. Many employees are bullied into believing that they must take their money, which is simply not true.

Third, if they are not eligible to contribute to your plan for one year, remind them that they can contribute to an IRA and receive a full deduction; the inability to contribute is not as large an opportunity cost as it might otherwise seem.

In fact, employees are often too anxious to roll over money that would be better off in a rollover IRA. An employee's own IRA with a collection of pure no-load mutual funds will often provide infinite investment flexibility compared to a 401(k) plan that has a limited choice of investments and administrative costs that are passed on to the employee.

Ideally, an employee should roll over old account balances into a new employer's 401(k) plan only when the employee wants to access the funds through the 401(k) plan loan provision, which is not available with an IRA.

Fourth, when employees do become eligible for your plan, even if only in the fourth quarter of the year, they can contribute up to 25% of their entire year's compensation. For example, an employee making $40,000 by year-end could, in theory, deposit the entire $10,000 that he or she earns during the fourth quarter.

Restricting Eligibility and Safe Harbor Provisions

Restricted eligibility reduces the cost of safe harbor contributions. (As discussed in Chapter 10, the safe harbor approach allows 401(k) testing to be ignored if the company contributed specified amounts into the plan.)

Eligibility will become increasingly important for plans attempting to meet the safe harbor requirement with company contributions. Limiting the number of employees who will receive these company contributions will substantially reduce the cost and increase the probability that the safe harbor approach will be a viable option.

Summary

One key to designing an effective 401(k) plan are eligibility requirements: the eligibility period and which employees will be eligible to participate. The objective is to include employees more likely to contribute and exclude those less likely to contribute.

Choosing correct eligibility requirements lays a solid foundation for a smooth-running plan that passes tests and meets expectations. Also, more restrictive eligibility reduces the administrative costs of processing short-term employees.

Restrict the Eligibility Period

- The eligibility period is the length of time that an employee must work before being eligible to join the 401(k) plan.
- The most typical eligibility period is one year, although a shorter period may be advisable when the plan is just getting started.
- When eligibility periods of less than one year are used, plan sponsors must be aware of the *ripple effects*, such as needing to include part-time or seasonal workers.
- Pension law allows a company to set up two 401(k) plans, each having a different eligibility period, and this technique gives the plan sponsor design flexibility.

Restrict the Employees Who Are Eligible to Join the Plan

- Pension law allows companies to exclude (or *carve out*) up to 30% of their workers from being eligible for the plan. The percentage of non-highly compensated employees covered under the plan must be at least 70% of the percentage of highly compensated employees covered under the plan. For example, if 100% of a company's HCEs are covered, which is typical, then 70% of the NHCEs must be covered, and 30% can be carved out.
- Plan sponsors can choose to carve out HCEs, NHCEs, and employees in separate lines of business. Typically, employees who are under collective bargaining contracts are carved out; however, if a union agrees, unionized employees can be included.
- Leased employees may be included in a plan, but given the complexities involved, this should be very carefully examined.

PART 4
Creating the Ideal 401(k) Plan

PART FOUR BRINGS TOGETHER all of the elements discussed in this book—the legal requirements, cost considerations, administration, and investment services. It shows how to use these elements to design the ideal plan for a variety of organizations.

Chapter 12

Design Fine Points

CHAPTER 2 DISCUSSED two basic rules for designing a simple 401(k) plan: allow loans for any purpose and do not include matching contributions. This chapter covers six additional rules, as well as the pitfalls to avoid in the design process.

To keep the plan effective:

1. Operate the plan on a calendar year whenever possible.
2. Promote the plan every year.
3. Use popular mutual funds for the investment choices.
4. Do not underestimate employee sophistication and desire to save.
5. Promote and design the plan simultaneously.
6. Communicate by every means possible.

Operate On a Calendar Year

Choosing a calendar year for the 401(k) plan makes sense for several reasons. First, participants think and budget based on calendar years.

Second, if a 401(k) plan's year ends, for instance, on June 30, the plan straddles two calendar years, which can make solving any problems more costly—problems such as returning excess contributions to highly compensated employees because their plan failed an ADP Test. The following examples show how much easier it is to correct such a problem when the plan uses a calendar year.

Assumption: During the year, an executive contributes the maximum dollar amount of $10,000 to the 401(k) plan.

Example A—401(k) Plan Year: January 1–December 31, 1999
1. In January 2000 after the end of the 401(k) plan's year, it fails an ADP Test and returns as taxable income $240 of the executive's contributions plus investment income.
2. The plan must return money on a first-in-first-out basis, so the $240 is assumed to have been the first money contributed to the plan, in January 1999.
3. On April 15, 2000, the executive files his or her 1999 tax return reflecting the added taxable income. There is minimal inconvenience, and the tax return is filed at the normal time.

Example B—401(k) Plan Year: July 1, 1999–June 30, 2000
1. On April 15, 2000, the executive files a tax return for the 1999 tax year reflecting the contributions to the 401(k) plan made during 1999.
2. After the plan's year ends on June 30, 2000, the plan fails an ADP Test and must return, as in Example A, $240 plus investment income to the executive.
3. The money being returned to the executive must be considered the first contributed to the plan, in July 1999, the beginning of the 401(k) plan's year.
4. The executive filed his or her 1999 tax return three months earlier and now must refile the tax return.

In the second example, the executive is probably annoyed and blames the plan's administrator for not projecting more accurately or at least more conservatively how much could be contributed.

However, projections can never be totally accurate; the only test that can be accurate and the only test that counts is conducted at the end of the plan's year, when every dime of contributions from every eligible employee has been determined. And in a small company, testing can be dramatically affected when a few major participants leave the company or become eligible in midyear.

However, some 401(k) plans must operate on the company's non-calendar fiscal year, because the 401(k) plan has been added to an existing profit-sharing plan. Historically, a retirement plan's year usually coincided with the company's fiscal year; contributions could be calculated more easily. Any advantage this might provide today is far outweighed by the difficulties created, such as those illustrated in the examples on the previous page. Therefore, a calendar year for a 401(k) plan is strongly recommended.

Promote the Plan Every Year

Employees need to be reminded periodically of the plan's accomplishments. 401(k) plans compete with all the other ways that people are tempted to spend money. As new employees become eligible, they should receive not just a package of written 401(k) materials and an enrollment form, but also a sales talk.

The plan's best salespeople can often be the company's in-house contact person (the office manager or human resources manager) as well as the employees' supervisors. Some companies pay bonuses to supervisors based on how many of their subordinates contribute to the 401(k) plan. This one-time or periodic bonus, involving just a few hundred dollars per manager, is often more effective and much cheaper than a matching contribution.

When promoting a plan, then, be creative. Some firms use posters in the cafeteria, a mention in the monthly newsletter, a chart on the wall showing how the investments are doing, and so on. Anything goes.

Some sage once said, *Good ideas are a dime a dozen, but it's only the ones that get sold that are worth anything.* You can't put a 401(k) plan on automatic pilot and expect it to promote itself.

Use Popular Mutual Funds As Investments

Mutual funds are the investment of choice for a well-run 401(k) plan. Some plans have experimented with so-called *wrap accounts* that use individual money managers and invest in individual securities. But compared to mutual funds, wrap accounts have several disadvantages.

First, they cost about 3% per year, which is subtracted from earnings. (Chapter 5 discusses the need to keep internal costs low.)

Second, wrap accounts, or any pool of money other than mutual funds, cannot be followed in the newspaper by participants and are not ranked by any of the standard mutual fund ranking services. This takes away some of the excitement of investing, and thus of participating in the plan.

Finally, the accounting and auditing of mutual funds is easier (and ultimately cheaper) because the funds do all the work.

Mutual funds represent the investment of choice for 401(k) plans with less than $10 million in assets. If plan sponsors don't use them, frustration and/or unnecessary expense will likely result.

Do Not Underestimate Employees' Readiness to Save

Many company owners and senior managers believe that rank-and-file employees live from paycheck to paycheck and can never save any money. Just such a sentiment was expressed by the president of a San Francisco bank who said, "We have a lot of single mothers as tellers. We make it a point to hire them because they are such motivated workers. I can't imagine that they will be able to afford very much in the way of contributions."

For my own edification, I sat down with the bank's personnel officer after the enrollment process. The single mothers, who we identified as a group, were contributing an average of 13% of their pay!

By the same token, Hispanic workers have a tremendous reputation for contributing large amounts to 401(k) plans. Mexico has one of the highest per capita savings rates of any industrialized nation. That instinct to save translates into high 401(k) participation rates from Hispanic workers here in the United States. Yet, in many companies whose workforce consists of a large proportion of foreign nationals, plan sponsors operate on the misconception that non-English-speaking employees will not participate in a 401(k) plan.

One way to avoid these misconceptions is to discuss with employees the possibility of offering a 401(k) plan before the plan design is complete.

Promote and Design Simultaneously

Promoting the plan and designing the plan are part of the same exercise, and should be done at the same time.

All too often, a 401(k) consultant will use census information on a group of employees to generate what is supposedly an ideal plan design for that group. Usually this pre-designed plan includes a matching provision and some estimates of its cost based on estimated employee contributions. But no one has a clue about the likely participation and contribution rates in the specific company.

Asking the Employees

In a smaller company (fewer than 50–75 employees), plan sponsors can adopt a wait-and-see approach about eligibility and other design components, and make a final decision after seeing how many and which employees wish to participate.

The presentation of the plan can be prefaced by pointing out that no final decision has been made about offering the plan. However, if enough employees express an interest, the company will then pay to have the plan installed and administered.

There is probably a psychological advantage gained by suggesting that a benefit will not be offered unless there is enough participation. As human beings, we all are inclined to be more interested in something that is not automatically handed to us. Also, some peer pressure will be brought to bear if some employees really want the plan and realize that they have to talk it up with their fellow workers before it can happen.

In some cases, plan sponsors may find that a handful of relatively new employees would like to make substantial contributions. These may be employees who would not have qualified under a one-year waiting period. As discussed in Chapter 11, beginning the plan with an eligibility period of less than one year (to include these high contributors) may generate a better test in the first year. Thereafter, a one-year eligibility period could be installed for all new employees.

The Mistake of Sending a Memo

Caution: don't let the decision to install a plan hinge on a memo passed out to employees. Some employers say that they have taken a *survey* and nobody is interested in a 401(k) plan. The survey is often nothing more than the question, *Do you want the company to take some money out of your pay for a savings plan?* Products and services are not sold this way, and neither is a 401(k) plan.

Make sure that employees are *voting* based on a substantive and full presentation of the plan.

In some cases, a plan is designed best when the design and promotion are combined, turning the employee promotional meeting into a fact-finding session. Explain the plan to employees in its simplest form and use the enrollment exercise to gauge the level of interest. The process of designing and promoting moves ahead in a tandem fashion, which leads to an optimal plan from the standpoint of participation and company cost.

Use All Means to Communicate

The three primary rules of successful promotion are:

1. Communication
2. Communication
3. Communication

Employee educational materials come in a wide variety of forms today. Some vendors have excellent materials, but it is always worth reviewing what independent educational companies offer. The price may not be that great and in some cases the vendor will pay for whatever you insist upon.

Videotapes are very important because employees under about age 40 generally don't read as much as older workers; they get most of their sensory and educational input from television and computer screens. Several companies offer videotapes that are engaging and effective. Money Insights (phone 800-858-6663) is an example of a company that offers educational packages including standard and customized videotapes and corresponding printed information. Their tapes are modular (plans with loans, plans with no loans, plans with a match, plans with no match, and so on), and they are available in both English and Spanish.

Most financial institutions offer tapes and written material that are too dumbed down to be effective. The materials have been distilled through the legal department and various committees to the extent that they have been neutered of much valuable content. By comparison, the tapes made by independents work, and they are entertaining. For example, some major chain stores creating 401(k) plans have thrown away the free tapes and use the Money Insights tapes exclusively, because contribution levels in some cases increased by a factor of four.

All vendors of educational material will send their samples for a free preview. Every plan sponsor should consider something beyond what the vendor provides. The results can be astounding.

The Internet is on its way. Many vendors have Internet capabilities, which further aid in communication. The primary advantage of the Internet, however, is that participant balances can be presented on the screen, which can be more user friendly than hearing recorded messages about account balances on an 800 line.

Companies such as Financial Engines are offering sophisticated asset allocation models for serious 401(k) enthusiasts who want to effectively place their accounts on the Internet and let Financial Engines rebalance and continually update the allocation. This is a service that requires cooperation (and money) from the plan sponsor before it can be a reality for the employee.

Fast-growing companies such as The Scarborough Group bypass the plan sponsor completely. Participants pay a flat annual fee of $325 for end-to-end retirement plan management, including customized education, objective asset allocation advice, and discretionary management of funds. Participants work directly with a personal Retirement Advisor who proactively allocates plan assets to reach the retirement goals established collaboratively with the participant. The Scarborough Group's sister company, Scarborough Retirement Services, works with plan sponsors to offer a similar service. There is definitely an argument for hiring these independent advisory companies. Quality, price, and extent of the service can be controlled more effectively than with a built-in component of bundled services.

Let me add two final elements of investment education. First, the Appendix to this book contains ten key concepts that plan participants should consider when selecting investments. For those plan sponsors wanting to provide this basic information to their employees, just copy this list verbatim or download an expanded list from the web site: www.pensiondynamics.com.

Second, for those plan participants really serious about investing, I suggest three books:

> *Bogle On Mutual Funds* by John Bogle, founder of the Vanguard family of funds. This is one of the best books ever written about mutual funds. It is written with a very objective viewpoint and is easy to read. Sophisticated financial information is presented in an understandable format.

> *Mutual Funds For Dummies* by Eric Tyson. The title says it all.

> *Why Smart People Make Big Money Mistakes* by Gary Belsky and Thomas Gilovich. This is a highly readable account of the research in behavioral economics. It explains how investors think and why built-in human behavior naturally leads to bad investment decisions. This book is a potent weapon in the battle of mind over money, and every 401(k) participant should read it.

These independent services and sources fill a need that the financial institutions just cannot meet for reasons having to do with their fiduciary paranoia.

Avoid Design Pitfalls

All too often, the installation of 401(k) plans is unnecessarily delayed, or even derailed, in the design stage by a mistaken focus on three issues:

1. Choosing investments
2. Calculating the cost of a matching provision under varying scenarios
3. Trying to minimize participant borrowing

The cause of this mistaken focus: choosing the wrong type of organization to help design the plan.

Investment People Are Not Always the Best Designers

A financial institution that sells investments is not always the best designer of a 401(k) plan. The institution wants as much money as possible contributed to the plan, so it naturally tries to sell the employer on a matching contribution, even though a plan might be very successful without one. The substantial cost of a matching contribution may prompt employers to delay the plan or not offer it at all.

As a pension administrator, I have been amazed at how many companies of 25–75 employees have no pension or 401(k) plan. In most cases, the reason given is, *We couldn't afford a matching contribution, and everyone said it wouldn't work without a matching provision*. In these situations, I have always been able to install a 401(k) plan without a matching provision. In cases where the testing results fell a little short, my clients (the company owners) could only contribute $5,000 a year instead of their full $10,000. I would argue that the plan is still worth the investment.

In addition to wanting as much money as possible contributed to the plan, financial institutions want as little money as possible to be taken out of the plan. I often see financial institutions suggesting that loans be limited to a far greater extent than the law requires. The reason, of course, is that loans reduce money under management and are competition for the investments that the financial institution tries to sell. This is a double-edged sword because investment institutions do not appreciate that a liberal loan provision clears the way for larger contributions to the plan and, ultimately, more money for investments.

Traditional Pension Administrators Also Are Not Ideal Designers

Traditional pension administration companies often have trouble with 401(k) plans.

Many administration companies have been slow to recognize the differences between 401(k) plans and conventional pension plans. For example, in a conventional pension plan, all investment decisions are made by the trustees, and participants receive annual statements well after the end of the year—statements that tell them their contributions, vested amount, and total account balance. If a participant leaves a company and has a vested account balance to be paid out, the pension administrator can conduct the payout in a leisurely fashion, taking as long as 18 months from the date of termination.

By comparison, an administrator of a 401(k) plan typically generates quarterly reports to participants. These participants see, and occasionally change, their investment mix. They can borrow from their accounts, and if they leave the company, they will want their money immediately—not a year or so after their termination date.

Some pension administration firms have gravitated more easily toward 401(k) plans. The plan sponsor should choose a firm based upon its 401(k) reputation. The number of plans the firm has designed is probably the best measure of competence.

Summary

If plan sponsors appreciate the complexity of the design process, they will understand that the greatest ongoing cost of a 401(k) plan could be the opportunity cost of a missing design component that would have made the plan more cost efficient. These plans are not cookie-cutter commodities. Every company's demographics, and therefore its needs, are different, and these differences should be reflected in the design of the 401(k) plan.

Here is a good rule of thumb about plan design: in the beginning, keep the plan as simple as possible and as exclusive as possible. After a year or so, improve it (as to coverage testing) by allowing more employees to be eligible. Or add a small matching contribution; then, and only then, should this additional element and its cost to the plan be considered.

Adhering to these design tips will improve the probability of a trouble-free plan with high satisfaction among rank and file employees and some powerful tax benefits for owners and senior managers.

To paraphrase from the film *Field of Dreams: If you build it, they will come*. To get employees to come to a 401(k) plan, the plan sponsor should keep the plan simple.

Operate the Plan On a Calendar Year

- The 401(k) plan does not need to operate on the same year as the company.
- Using a non-calendar year causes major complications if contributions ever need to be returned to participants.

Promote the Plan Every Year

- New employees must be sold on the plan.
- Assign responsibility for the sales effort to specific employees, such as supervisors.

Use Popular Mutual Funds for Investment Choices

- Mutual funds perform their own accounting and auditing functions, thus reducing the cost of using them.
- Participants can keep up with their investments on a daily basis through newspapers and mutual fund rating services, thus increasing the excitement of investing.

Do Not Underestimate Employees' Desire to Save

- Avoid misconceptions about employee attitudes.
- Employees today want to save, if not for retirement, for major purchases or college tuition.

Promote and Design the Plan Simultaneously

- Hold a meeting with employees to discuss the possibility of offering the plan and gauge employee interest.
- Modify the design of the plan based on feedback from employees.

Avoid Design Pitfalls

- Choose a plan designer based on the firm's reputation and experience with 401(k) plans.
- Be aware that financial institutions and traditional pension administration companies have biases that affect their recommendations about design, such as investment choices, matching contributions, and loan provisions.

Chapter 13

Pulling It All Together

DESIGNING THE RIGHT PLAN
FOR YOUR ORGANIZATION

Few situations lend themselves to perfect solutions, so designing a 401(k) plan is often an exercise of compromise to create
the greatest good for the greatest number. We are weaving together
a matrix of many factors and considerations. What is most important is that the matrix draws from the largest possible universe of
material in the form of investments, services, and ideas.

The purpose of this book is to contribute as much as possible to
the decision-making process—to offer a perspective that will lead
to informed decisions.

In designing the right plan for our organization, we begin by
conducting an appraisal of our *audience*. What kind of people do
we have in our company, and what type of 401(k) plan will best
meet what we assume are their needs?

The following companies offer three typical situations calling for
dramatically different approaches to plan design and vendor
selection.

Everyone Wins At a Small Professional Firm

A 50-employee law firm or engineering firm (possibly software
engineering) has a mix of owners, associates who are not owners,

and administrative people.

The groups are generally well paid. The owners have an average age of 55, associates an average of 45, and administrative staff an average of 35.

Because a number of partners have been with the firm for almost 20 years, the 401(k) plan is top heavy: these partners have over 60% of all assets in the plan (see Chapter 10 for the top-heavy discussion). This requires that the company make at least a 3% contribution for all non-highly compensated people in order for the partners to make 401(k) contributions themselves.

The partners elect to make a 3% company discretionary contribution (profit-sharing contribution) into the plan, instead of a matching contribution. As a special bonus, the 3% contribution meets the safe harbor requirement that does away with the need for passing the ADP Test, so all highly compensated employees can make their maximum 401(k) contributions, regardless of what testing might have dictated.

All employees receive this 3% discretionary contribution. It becomes the *base contribution*, because the company wants to contribute more into the accounts of the partners and associates. The company can do this by using one of two techniques: integrating the plan with Social Security or cross testing.

Integrating the Plan With Social Security

Companies can make an additional contribution of employees' earnings to the plan for earnings above the Social Security wage base of $72,600 (1999).

In this example, the company decides to contribute 3% (to repeat, this is in addition to the base contribution of 3%). Partners who have an average pay of $160,000 receive $2,622 ($160,000 minus $72,600 times 3%). The company's contribution to associates is calculated the same way: the difference between their pay and $72,600 times 3%. Since none of the administrative staff makes more than $72,600, they do not qualify for this contribution.

Using the Cross-Testing Technique

Alternately, the owners could decide to use a technique called *cross testing*. This allows owners to contribute different percentage amounts of pay to themselves, the associates, and the administrative staff. The administrative staff, for example, would get a lower percentage than the associates, who in turn would get less than the owners.

The law allows this differentiation of contributions, because the administrative staff (who are younger) will receive their contributions for longer periods of time than the older workers. So, the total dollars they receive will approximate the amount received by the associates and owners getting the higher percentage contributions.

Thus, the firm is divided into three groups. The administrative staff, who have an average of 30 years until retirement, receives their 3% base contribution. The associates, who are within 20 years of retirement, receive 4% in addition to the base 3% contribution (a total of 7%); and the partners, with just 10 years to go, receive 9% in addition to the 3% base (a total of 12%).

The effect of cross testing is striking. Assume that a partner who earns $160,000 makes a voluntary $10,000 contribution into the plan. Then, the company contributes an additional 12% of $160,000 ($19,200) into the plan. This brings the partner to almost $30,000 or the maximum individual contribution level.

An associate making $80,000 contributes $10,000 into the 401(k) and receives an additional company contribution of 7% or $5,600, for a total of $15,600.

To decide which is the better option, the discretionary contribution plus either cross testing or integrating the plan with Social Security, the company would simply run the numbers both ways.

Better Than a Bonus for the Administrative Staff

Even a member of the administrative staff making $33,333 does well. The 3% base discretionary contribution amounts to $1,000 (3% times $33,333). This is an improvement over any current taxable bonus of the same amount. If the staff member is contributing the maximum to the 401(k) and paying taxes on the taxable bonus at a rate of 42% (combined federal, state, and social security taxes), a

$1,000 bonus nets the employee only about $580.

Instead, the entire $1,000 goes into the 401(k) plan. In theory, employees who need the money can borrow half of this contribution, and be within a few dollars ($500 versus $580) of where they would have been if paid in taxable dollars. Now, however, they have the other half still in their plan, growing toward retirement. And the company saves money because a taxable bonus would have included payroll tax and workers compensation costs.

This Plan's Other Design Features

This plan's investments should probably be chosen from a large universe of funds to assure a reasonably sophisticated selection. A low cost to participants for these mutual funds should be paramount, because more than 60% of the plan's money is in the accounts of partners, so they are paying for the plan both as participants and as plan sponsors. It is far cheaper for them to pay for the plan with tax-deductible corporate dollars rather than with retirement plan earnings that could be compounding on a tax-deferred basis.

In this plan, daily valuation is not as important as getting good actuarial consulting for the cross-test formula.

Increasing Participation At a Medium-Sized Firm

A 200-employee manufacturing company with 175 non-union workers and 25 management people has a problem plan: it never passes its ADP Test. Highly compensated managers who would like to contribute more are frustrated in these efforts. How can plan participation be increased so the ADP Test can be passed?

The Key Is Communication

English is not a first language for many of the employees, so communication is paramount in this case. Videotapes explaining the plan in English and other languages can be purchased from independent communication companies (see Chapter 12). In addition, translators should be present for all employee meetings; Total Benefit Communications (phone 404-256-5042) provides 401(k) meetings in any language anywhere in the country.

The vendor chosen should have good educational materials offered in the languages necessary to meet the needs of employees.

If there is any case in which higher participant costs may be justified, this could be it. If a vendor offers to do individual employee meetings on a regular basis, this additional promotional effort and assistance for the employees can justify the extra cost. A high level of hands-on assistance is almost never available without an extra cost despite any promises that might have been made. (If participants are paying higher costs, make sure the higher level of service is still being delivered two or more years after the installation of the plan.)

Keeping Things Simple

The plan should be daily valued. This helps participants to feel a sense of immediacy and that the money is really theirs. Some foreign nationals have a basic distrust of financial institutions, because in some countries bank deposits are not federally guaranteed; the features of the plan need to be sensitive to this.

The emphasis should be on relatively simple investments, rather than anything complicated. The investments should be limited in number so that they can be easily explained.

If a group of employees in the company are less likely to participate, they should be carved out of the plan so they do not reduce the testing percentages. Carving out allows up to 30% of the workforce to be excluded from the plan. In this company, there may be a natural *break* in the workforce that allows this carve-out to take place without any adverse political fallout.

The *negative election* (see Chapter 9) is an ideal way to boost participation. This requires that employees fill out a form if they do not want to participate. Otherwise, some percentage of pay (you decide the amount) will automatically go into the plan beginning with the first pay period following their eligibility date. A typical negative election amount is 3% of pay. Depending upon the eligibility date, the negative election amount may coincide with a pay raise.

A relatively small match can go a long way toward boosting participation in this instance. Fifty cents for each dollar contributed up to a maximum match of, say, $200 per employee represents a relatively small cost when compared to total payroll. It can make it more difficult for an employee to not participate to at least some degree.

Making a Matching Contribution Work in a Large Firm

In a large 1,000-employee company spread out over several divisions, the top management at headquarters want a 401(k) plan for themselves with a matching or employer-discretionary contribution. But the cost of offering this throughout the company would be prohibitive.

The management ideally would like to offer a short eligibility period to recruit new management people, but the cost of shortening eligibility company wide would increase the cost and *hassle factor* of the plan and jeopardize what are now borderline testing results.

Divide and Conquer the Problem

So, we divide the company into two plans. The *haves*, so to speak, have the matching contribution, and the *have-nots* do not.

Fortunately, the portion of the company located outside of headquarters does, in fact, have some highly compensated employees. Thanks to coverage testing rules, these HCEs elsewhere in the company open the door to some creative design options.

Of some 50 highly compensated employees, 15 are in divisions of the company as managers or marketing people away from headquarters. If we carve them out and include just the 35 HCEs working at headquarters, we are covering only 70% of our highly compensated employees in the *matching* plan.

In calculating how many of the NHCEs must be covered in this plan, we know they must equal 70% of the percent of the company's HCEs who are covered. Therefore, 70% times 70% means that 49% of the company's NHCEs need to be covered by the matching plan. The two plans are tested separately, but only if the no-match plan also passes the coverage test. The no-match plan has 15 HCEs participating, out of a possible 50 HCEs—30%. Therefore, we need to make sure that out of the entire company, we have at least 21% (70% times 30%) of the NHCEs participating in this *no-match* plan.

In all, if at least 49% of the NHCEs participate in the match plan, and at least 21% of the NHCEs participate in the no-match plan, then the required 70% minimum is met for the organization as a whole.

The bottom line is that coverage testing becomes our friend in these large company situations. In my experience, some of the largest companies with relatively unsuccessful plans have had the least creativity applied to plan design. Many upper-level managers have lost valuable retirement savings opportunities as a result.

All too often, large companies have chosen their vendors based on characteristics such as employee educational materials and name-brand mutual funds. In most cases, the representatives from the financial institutions have been asset salespeople rather than pension professionals, and the low level of sophistication in many of these plans is a testament to this fact.

Other Design Features

The investments for this plan should be on one platform (one mutual fund family or one transfer agent) for ease of administration, and the plan should be valued daily. The latter is important because employees will interact directly with the financial institution rather than through the in-house contact person. The mutual funds should be chosen with an eye to their cost.

A compliance guarantee is especially important. Too often, in a large company, there is a natural tendency to go with name-brand financial institutions, which, unfortunately, are the least responsible if the ADP Test or Coverage Test is not performed properly. The costs of additional consulting and administration for this plan should be paid for as a deductible expense by the corporation.

An institutional trustee may also be a wise investment in this situation, because most management people will not want to volunteer to self-trustee a large plan. Trustee chores mainly require signing authorization letters for loans and distributions, but it is the fear of the unknown that prompts most managers of large corporations to resist taking on this role. Again, the fact that there is an institutional trustee and a CPA firm auditing the plan each year does not excuse the plan sponsor from any compliance responsibility. Keeping the plan in compliance with tax laws is solely the company's responsibility, unless it has specifically contracted that role out to an independent organization.

Here then, within one company, we have opened the door to creating a plan for management that serves different constituencies in different ways. It may be more expensive than the current plan, but weighed against the cost of all the income taxes that could otherwise be contributed to retirement plans, the additional cost represents a tremendous value. At least the cost of offering the matching benefit to non-management employees has been reduced by half, thanks to our carve-out efforts. Further work in plan design could go toward creating an ideal plan for management and an improved, cost-effective compensation component for at least half of the remaining employees.

Seize the Chance to Customize Your 401(k) Plan

These three plans spotlight the application of the tools and techniques spelled out earlier in this book. To create a successful 401(k) plan, the keys are to recognize what is important to a specific workforce, and to discern how different plan design and vendor combinations best complement a company's compensation objectives.

Try to maintain a plan that offers the greatest savings opportunity to the greatest number of employees. These are people who are saving money that would otherwise have disappeared in taxes, and they are creating wealth more rapidly than through any other investment mechanism offered by our current legislative framework.

Football players learn that every play presented by the coach in a chalk talk with Xs, Os, and arrows will theoretically lead to a touchdown. Linemen memorize who they are supposed to block and runners memorize what they are supposed to do when any play is called. We all know, however, that almost anything can happen after the ball is snapped.

Too many 401(k) plans look great on paper, but the execution leaves them short of the goal line year after year. The purpose of this book is to focus you on the pivotal decision-making points that contribute the most toward the success of a plan. A five-star 401(k) in place of a mediocre one can mean millions of extra dollars to you and your fellow employees—and I mean a million dollars each in some cases. Self-serving advice or a lack of good advice from 401(k) vendors can stand in the way of what everyone wants: a smooth-running, profitable plan offering the law's maximum opportunities to save.

Anyone reading this book should consider its information to be like arrows in a quiver. If you see some information that would enhance your company's plan, don't hesitate to let management know about it. As an elderly husband once said to his wife, *Dear, you wish we were rich; why didn't you tell me that thirty years ago?* You may not have thirty years for an improved plan to increase your retirement nest egg, but improvements over just a few years can make a difference, and the satisfaction of having an optimal plan can be its own reward.

Appendix

WHAT PLAN PARTICIPANTS
SHOULD KNOW ABOUT INVESTING

THIS APPENDIX is a short but comprehensive list of key investment concepts. If a company has offered participants some version of this appendix and makes available some diskettes and videotapes, it would be difficult to argue that investment education has not taken place. You can lead a horse to water, but you can't make it drink, so to speak. If employers take the steps outlined here, they should have a clear conscience about the employees' education requirements, and they have probably limited their liability as much as it can be.

Rule #1

Higher rates of return create a lot more money. Earning just a few percentage points more per year on your 401(k) money makes a big difference at retirement.

If you contribute $5,000 per year to your 401(k) and earn 5% in a money market fund, you will have $63,000 in ten years. If you invest in stock funds that earn 10%, you will have $80,000 in ten years, almost $20,000 more.

In twenty years, your $5,000 per year in a 5% money market fund will have grown to $165,000, but your stock funds at 10%

would have increased to $285,000 . . . a difference of $120,000 in just twenty years, and a difference of $300,000 in thirty years.

Rule #2

The stock market is a proven winner. Over time, the stock market's rate of return has averaged six percentage points per year more than the return on money market funds.

Rule #3

The market is guaranteed to fluctuate. Stocks don't go up every year. During long periods of time, the stock market has had a 10% loss or *correction* every four years and a 20% loss every seven years. While average returns may be six percentage points better than money market funds, we need to remember that sooner or later we are guaranteed to lose money in the stock market for a while. This explains why the stock market cannot be used to save money for a short-term financial goal of less than five to seven years.

Rule #4

Given enough time, your stock market results will be positive. With few exceptions, the stock market has almost always made a profit during any ten-year period of time. If you had deposited money into the market on almost any day in this century and taken it back ten years later, you would have made money even if the ten-year period had included the Depression of the 1930s.

Rule #5

Chasing last year's best mutual fund is not a good strategy. While the average stock mutual fund has made more than 10% per year during the past ten years, the average mutual fund investor has made less than 3%. Most people are investing in the wrong mutual fund at the wrong time and cashing out after it drops in value. This is called *chasing last year's best performing fund*.

Rule #6

Staying with a strategy leads to success over time. The biggest risk investors face is the risk of abandoning their strategies. There are many different investment strategies, and almost all of them work if we have the discipline to stay with the one we have selected for ourselves. People lose money when they try to switch horses in midstream, or when they try to *time the market*.

Rule #7

The market is like a tide . . . raising and lowering all the ships. Roughly 70% of any one mutual fund's performance is a result of the entire stock market's performance. If the whole stock market is going up in value, there is a 70% chance that your mutual funds— no matter which ones you have chosen—will also be going up in value. The stock market over long periods of time has always increased in value, so this would indicate that the specific mutual funds you choose may not be that important in the long run.

Rule #8

Investment style is the second most important influence on returns. Different types of funds perform better or worse during different portions of an economic cycle. One month we might read that mutual funds with high tech stocks are doing well. Eight months later, funds with large blue chip stocks like General Motors and utility companies are performing better than all other kinds of mutual funds. The skill of the mutual fund managers has less to do with the performance of a fund than the type of investment style that the fund adopts.

Rule #9

A technique called *dollar-cost-averaging* is one of the best systems for beating the market—a powerful tool for achieving positive investment results. When we deposit the same amount of money each month into our 401(k), it actually helps us to have the market drop periodically. Our dollars simply buy more shares when those shares have dropped to lower prices. Later, when the shares have regained their value, we will have automatically bought shares at earlier, lower prices. Dollar-cost-averaging happens automatically thanks to the nature of monthly 401(k) deposits, and it increases the possibility of buying low and selling high.

Rule #10

Create your individual *path of minimum regret*. A mix of investment types creates a path of minimum regret and can lead to greater success over time. If you mix investment types when choosing stock mutual funds, this diversification will *smooth out* your investment performance. Figure A.1 shows how this diversification looks when graphed:

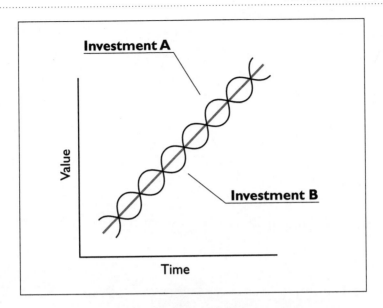

Figure A.1 The Path of Minimum Regret

The combined average result of all your funds will look more like a straight line than any one fund, and this reduced volatility will enable you to stick to your original strategy without losing sleep.

Keep these ten rules in mind when choosing your investment mix. Remember, your biggest risk as a 401(k) investor is the risk of abandoning your strategy. So choose your strategy carefully and then adjust it only as you approach the different goals you are using your 401(k) to achieve. Remember, today's long-term goal is tomorrow's short-term goal. In a perfect world, this steady compression of the time frame is the only event that should lead to a change in mix.

Notes

....

PREFACE

1. Michelle Andrews, "401(k) Crusaders," *Smart Money*, March 1999, p. 106.

2. Penelope Wang, "Protect Yourself Against Retirement Plan Ripoff," *Money*, April 1997, pp. 96–102.

3. E. S. Browning and Stephen Frank, "Winding Up Rich—Retirement Accounts Stashed In Stocks Make Employees Millionaires," *The Wall Street Journal*, July 7, 1997, p. 1.

CHAPTER 4

1. *Plan Sponsor* is published ten times a year by Asset International, Greenwich, CT. *The 401(k) Plan Answer Book*, by Joan Gucciardi, Steven J. Franz, Joan C. McDonagh, and John Michael Maier, is published by Panel Publishers, Inc., New York. *Tax Facts* is published by The National Underwriter Company, Cincinnati, OH. *401(k) Advisor* and *Pension Benefits* are published by Panel Publishers (a division of Aspen Publishers, Inc.), New York.

CHAPTER 5

1. Penelope Wang, "Protect Yourself Against Retirement Plan Ripoff," *Money*, April 1997, p. 101.

2. D. Hendricks, J. Patek, R. Zeckhauser, "Hot Hands In Mutual Funds: Short Run Persistence of Relative Performance, 1974–1988," *The Journal of Finance*, July 1993, p. 93.

CHAPTER 8

1. Neil Weinberg, "The House Take," *Forbes*, July 4, 1994, p. 151.

2. J. C. Bogle, *Bogle on Mutual Funds: New Perspectives for the Intelligent Investor.* (New York: Dell Publishing, 1994), p. 198.

CHAPTER 8

1. Neil Weinberg, "The House Take," *Forbes*, July 4, 1994, p. 151.

2. J. C. Bogle, *Bogle on Mutual Funds: New Perspectives for the Intelligent Investor.* (New York: Dell Publishing, 1994), p. 198.

Index

About the Author

Stephen J. Butler

M R. BUTLER IS currently the President and Cofounder of Pension Dynamics Corporation, a regional pension consulting and administration firm in the San Francisco Bay Area. He has worked in the pension and employee benefits area since the early 1970s, and has been credited with some of the earlier Employee Stock Ownership Plans and 401(k) plans installed in northern California.

A graduate of Harvard College (B.A. class of '66), Mr. Butler then attended the University of California Graduate School of Business Administration at Berkeley. Prior to receiving a degree, he left to serve on active duty for the United States Army as an officer in the Medical Services Corps during the Vietnam era, and later returned to civilian life to work for the Provident Mutual Life Insurance Company. In 1974, he cofounded an employee benefits company, Porter, Butler, Weber.

In 1980, he cofounded Pension Dynamics Corporation, which, since 1984, has specialized in designing and installing 401(k) plans. Operating as a so-called third-party administrator, Mr. Butler's company has remained independent of major financial institutions such as banks, insurance companies, and stock brokerage firms. This independence has set the stage for offering pure no-load funds as investment choices for plans which, in turn, has contributed to the popularity of such plans.

Within the pension industry, where he is a popular speaker, Steve Butler is best known as a leading advocate of cost-effective 401(k) plans. In case anyone misses the point, his California automobile license plate reads "MR 401K."

The author's family includes his wife, Frances, who is a psychi-atric social worker (MSW and Licensed Family Therapist). She maintains a private practice counseling victims of family violence. Their children include a daughter, Elsa, who is a graduate of Colorado College, and son, Mason, who attends the University of Colorado.

Mr. Butler's other interests include skiing, tennis, golf, sailing, motor cycling, furniture making, and playing bass violin in a jazz trio. As a triathelete, he is a three-time "escapee" from Alcatraz Island in San Francisco Bay.

He can be reached at the following:

Pension Dynamics Corporation
985 Moraga Road, Suite 210
Lafayette, California 94549
Telephone: (925) 299-8080
Email: PDC@value.net
Web site: http://www.pensiondynamics.com/index.html